6.?13.78

What's the best vacation for you? Does it suit your needs for independence, luxury or company? Is this the right time to go or are you too anxious or exhausted to relax?

"Vacationing is an art," according to Drs. Shapiro and Tuckman, and getting the emotions right is far more important to this art than packing the right wardrobe. In TIME OFF, a psychotherapist and a psychiatrist offer a set of guidelines designed to ensure your vacation pleasure — whether it be on a long weekend, two weeks by the sea, or three in Europe. Drs. Shapiro and Tuckman show how to choose a vacation—getting in touch with personal needs, sifting fact from fantasy and balancing expectations of grandeur and fine weather with reality. They point out the hidden spoilers (over-idealization, separation anxiety, guilt) that can ruin any holiday and show how different vacations bring different rewards—from a week at a plush resort to a ten-day round at a tennis camp.

(continued on back flap)

STEVE SHAPIRO is a psychotherapist and director of the Volunteer Counseling Service of Rockland County, an agency founded by the Ford Foundation to aid clients of Family Court. Dr. Shapiro received his Ph.D. in English from the University of Washington in 1965, and then taught literature and psychology from 1965 to 1970 at the University of California, Irvine. He is co-author of *Trusting Yourself: Psychotherapy as a Beginning* and *Feeling Safe: Making Space for the Self*. Dr. Shapiro lives in New City, New York, with his wife, Bonnie.

ALAN TUCKMAN is in private psychiatric practice and is associated with the Rockland County Community Mental Health Center. He graduated from Alfred University and the Chicago Medical School, was a resident in internal medicine and then in psychiatry at Downstate Medical Center and Brookdale Hospital. Dr. Tuckman is on the teaching faculty of Columbia University College of Physicians and Surgeons and lives in New City, New York, with his wife, Ellen, and their children.

(continued from front flap)

Too often a vacation is second best: it's two weeks planned without an afternoon to relax, let alone time and space to unwind. Or you feel guilty and take the children along or decide to see Rome when you want and need to go skiing. But vacations are also one of the few opportunities for recapturing those uncluttered and free moments of childhood when playful learning about the world and self was the only real necessity. TIME OFF is a guide that will show every perspective traveler how to take advantage of those opportunities.

TIME OFF

Time Off

A Psychological Guide to Vacations

STEPHEN A. SHAPIRO, Ph.D.

ALAN J. TUCKMAN, M.D.

Anchor Press / Doubleday
Garden City, New York 1978

This is the first edition of *Time Off*

Anchor Books edition: 1978

Library of Congress Cataloging in Publication Data

Shapiro, Stephen.
  Time off.

  Includes index.
  1. Leisure—United States—Psychological aspects.
2. Vocations—Psychological aspects. I. Tuckman,
Alan J., joint author. II. Title.
GV53.S46   790
ISBN: 0-385-12389-2
Library of Congress Catalog Card Number 76-42392

For the people who share our pleasures with us:
our wives and our friends

CONTENTS

INTRODUCTION

Americans are vacation-conscious people, and it would appear that the challenge of a vacation is far greater for Americans than for anyone else. We have more free time available today than ever before. There are more places for us to go. There is more money for us to go with. There are more things for us to do.

In reality, however, there is also a possibility that America is a nation whose people have forgotten how to play. Free time is filled more with maintaining and repairing the products of a complex existence than with their enjoyment. People spend their days off washing the car, painting the house, cutting the grass, sealing the boat and performing all the other upkeep functions required to maintain their possessions in working order.

For many, such activities are relaxing. How many people blissfully declare, "I get my kicks out of just puttering around the house"? But Thoreau was speaking for the majority when he said, "Our things own us and we live lives of quiet desperation." It is a desperation that results from being trapped within a circle of mechanical "get away" devices whose incessant demands on the time and energy of their owners keeps them from ever truly getting away.

Even when the sailboats, the snowmobiles and the dune buggies all work, their owners are often seduced into an attitude of "simultaneous consumption" just to get it all in. This attitude is a pervasive one. Children watch television while doing their homework and while wolfing their dinners from TV tables. Adults might be reading the paper, listening to the radio, writing up a last report and planning their activities for the following day, all at the same time.

This frantic quality of activities persists on holidays as well. Modern vacations mean sight-seeing, shopping, games and a whole complex of endeavors that ultimately make the leisure period more utilitarian, more competitive, more jampacked with too many rituals of conspicuous consumption. The real goal, underneath it all, is not to make time off as much like every other moment of their daily lives as possible. But they are sometimes too caught up in the game to see the point.

Things have become so central to desires that people ignore or minimize all other needs. They work long hours because overtime means more money and more purchasing power and, therefore, more possessions. Vacations—the alternative—mean recreation, rest and perhaps quiet, but are often the overdue rewards that one puts off until the house gets painted, work quiets down, etc. Free time is not looked upon as essential and is played like a bargaining chip, either between union and management on the job or (more usually) within the individual debating over personal goals.

Here the literature of industrial and personal psychology

has been seriously deficient. Until recently, studies have neg-
lected the fact that leisure is as real a human requirement as
any other. But within the last few years there has been an
effort to fill this gap. Several universities have even established
Leisure Science departments to study the meanings and implications of free time. Findings are still tentative, but certain di-
rections have begun to appear. Scientists meeting at the National Conference on the Mental Health Aspects of Sports,
Exercise and Recreation sponsored by the American Medical
Association in 1975 were virtually unanimous in concluding
that relaxation and stimulation are essential to health and continued psychological renewal.

Most investigators also agree that, while people all need success on the job to improve their self-esteem, they become confused at the end of each year if their effort has not produced
the emotional pay-off they had anticipated. Their confusion
leads to alienation, frustration and stress. By then the tension
has piled high, and the typical reaction is to push ahead, to
continue working—working harder if possible—in the vain
hope that all the disagreeable feelings might be pushed out of
the way, if only one plows through them.

Unfortunately, this remedy doesn't work. The sum of all
the real and imaginary pressures of the job is found in the
statistics of all those who must seek outside help for a wide variety of stress-related symptoms, symptoms that cannot be ex-
plained by their working conditions alone. Headaches, insom-
nia, irritability, family conflict, alcoholism: These may be
the prices people pay for living under an unrelieved cloud of
tension.

What is suggested by all of this is that if the pace of time is
becoming so unavoidably furious, then it should be increas-

ingly vital to structure that time in the most beneficial manner possible. To contribute toward this end, the vacation period must be made as valuable and as fulfilling as it can to help achieve a greater tolerance of the accelerated pace of modern life. Otherwise, the tensions magnify and the stresses get out of control. Then the brittleness of a person's tolerance can become such a central fact of personality that there will be a danger of shattering with every step. Vacationing in this taut world is not a luxury; it is a necessity.

But it is not easy to find the right vacation. Holiday success is *not* based on flying off to some deluxe resort or on spending a lot of money or on anything so concrete. A receptive, emotionally healthy vacationer can find a rewarding and fully satisfying experience at home or virtually anyplace else, while another, trapped by inappropriate emotions or by poor preparations, can be miserable even in the "best" surroundings. Whether it is sight-seeing in Europe or camping in the United States, spending a week with relatives or a month traveling cross-country, the success of the experience—how well it is integrated with the rest of one's life—rests with the vacationer alone.

The art of vacationing—and it is an art—is further complicated by its image, by the common fantasy that others somehow manage to bring off the feat of enjoying themselves on holiday with remarkable ease. Many disillusioned travelers look at the tanned, healthy figures in the brochures and on the posters wishing that they could be like those ideal creatures—carefree and unlined. But that is just another part of the myth. Living is not like that. Those perfect specimens are not real people struggling with a real experience.

The true process of a holiday is never really easy and not always quite what it seems. It is an essential part of living, but it is also a process filled with complex ups and downs, and furthermore, it is like that for everyone. This book is an attempt to deal with that process as it is, stripped of its sometimes intimidating mystique. A real vacation is open to everyone as an opportunity to be enjoyed.

CHAPTER ONE

Play Is Serious Business

As they ready themselves for the coming holiday, most people will carefully plan when to go, what to take, where to stay, what to wear and how much money to carry. But rarely will they pause to consider those deeper questions that may also hold the fate of the holiday in a delicate balance. Few travelers ever wonder about their reasons for going in the first place, or ask themselves how their own special needs will be met when they get there. Or—perhaps most important of all— how they have meshed practical decisions with the facts and facets of their personalities.

Some naturally have an understanding of themselves and of their temperament, so they will plan vacations with a steady eye out for their real needs. But many others require a little more critical self-examination and an understanding of their goals before embarking on a two-week adventure. Some of these "others" will be fortunate and will return home refreshed and renewed: some, but not all. Not everyone can count on always doing the right thing and always making the right decision solely by intuition. For most people, in fact, the success or failure of a vacation undertaken without any sort of deeper planning becomes almost a whim of the gods. Advance attention to your personality as a traveler is a crucial ingredient to insuring that your next holiday is the glorious triumph you so richly deserve.

The suggestion of such planning may sound obvious. Holidays really are, in the old phrase, "the fruit of one's labor," so why would anyone not be ready for them? The attitude here answers the question: Since time off is such a natural and inevitable product of work anyway, why bother to make special preparations for it? It is as if one were to make special plans for the sun coming up tomorrow. The consequence of this approach is that returning vacationers surveyed by the Worldly Travelers Club confessed to disillusionment or even to open depression a full 60 per cent of the time. If this figure is even remotely true, it suggests that many holiday travelers are unsure of themselves, of their motives, of their expectations, or perhaps of all three. It further suggests that time off is taken too much for granted.

A vacation entails a challenge. For it often necessitates being able to shift from structured to unstructured time, from an intense routine of productivity to the alien life of leisure, from a diet of hasty dinnertime conversation to a long languid feast of intimacy. A more deliberate approach to vacations, which can make this transition less jagged and less of an afterthought, begins to sound more realistic.

Flexible planning can also serve as a guard against the unexpected; it can provide the traveler with an attitude that will make it easier to face the unknown. Consider the case of the three brothers who planned a vacation in Vermont together with their wives and children (six boys ranging in age from two and a half to seven). With the intention of recapturing the closeness they had felt for one another while growing up, they carefully selected a week at a small rural campground with cabins, volleyball, basketball and a tennis court. This setting provided ample opportunity for diversion for both the adults and the children, while at the same time offering the chance of shared experience for the three families.

Together, they spent long hours preparing for their adventure, deciding on a schedule of activities that covered everything from the amount of time the families should have to themselves to when the children should get together and when the adults would be alone. They called ahead to find out about baby-sitters, about local restaurants, even about alternate tennis courts should the one at the campsite prove too crowded. All of this planning, while keeping to the original purpose of spending time together, took into consideration everyone's individual needs and left sufficient room for moments of privacy and solitude.

They had prepared for everything, in fact, except rain. Which was just what they encountered: for five of the seven days they awakened to the sounds of a tropical downpour beating against the roof. There could be no tennis, no volleyball, no walks through the woods to see the wildlife, no picnics by the stream. Their imaginings had been outflanked by reality, and had they come to Vermont with their fantasies alone, the vacation would have been ended with its beginning. But these three families had a "tradition" of careful planning and flexibility.

So rather than giving up, rather than going home in disgust and disappointment, they simply modified their expectations. Instead of volleyball, there were excursions to local factories and workshops where they saw jams, leather goods, cheeses and snowshoes being made. Between the showers, there were opportunities for tennis on the all-weather town courts and some adventurous hikes along the banks of a raging mountain stream. In the evenings, baby-sitters allowed the adults to sample the country restaurants and take in a few movies. A potential disaster was thus converted into a memorable and rewarding week, an experience to remember and to treasure.

This vacation had succeeded despite the odds because of the planning that had gone into it. The consultations and discussions before leaving home had put these families in touch with their own feelings and desires—with their own *needs*—and they were quickly able to adjust their expectations to the unplanned reality they actually encountered.

As this experience shows, preparation need not be all-inclusive to be effective. It should be just enough to bring to the traveler the self-understanding that allows dealing with each new experience successfully, no matter how sudden, no matter how unforeseen.

It further suggests that going on a vacation is not just a matter of throwing some things together and taking off. The success or failure of any holiday depends less on the reality of the event than on the *sensibility* and *attitude* of the individual encountering that event. Getting the *emotions* right turns out to be far more important than packing the right wardrobe.

For play is serious business. Being successful at it means leaving routine behind and breaking some familiar ties. It means welcoming new "playmates" and tempering those facets of one's personality that are usually preoccupied with work and worry. Any holding back, clinging to feelings of uneasiness or even guilt about not working, causes a person to avoid the reality of play—that it requires full involvement. Interestingly, the word "play" derives from roots meaning to celebrate or to clap hands, and also to pledge and make a commitment. These clearly suggest group activities; you commit yourself to others, you pledge yourself to others. And you clap hands with others. And people are socialized to feel that playing *alone* is somehow incomplete. Also, the older one gets the more play becomes defined—as a tennis game, a hobby. The idea of stopping work and taking pleasure for the self alone—without the social commitment—is difficult for many and impossible for some.

Some people, although it may sound strange, are clearly afraid of even the possibility of pleasure, since they fear that it could leave them alone and adrift, without the comfort of a supporting cast. They are afraid of the possibility of exploring alternatives and the risk of engagement with strangers. So, locking themselves into a structure of relentless activity, many have delegated all pleasure and play to children. This "adult" view conveniently provides protection—an avoidance of emotional or physical involvement. Rejuvenation, both of themselves and of others, is neatly avoided and pleasure becomes ever more remote.

Real pleasure demands a full commitment to the experience.

It means being able to let go of cares, of worries, of thinking about other things. Like a perfect dive, pleasure requires a *plunging forth* as well as a *surrender*.

As we shall see, a vacation is one of the few opportunities available for recapturing those uncluttered and free moments of childhood when playful learning about the world and about the self was the only real necessity. A vacation is a private celebration that can lead to a rediscovery of the body, of forgotten physical skills, of social charms; perhaps it can even lead to a different attitude toward the life left at home. Vacation play is meant to exercise the stale regions of the self, to irrigate a desert and to make a private landscape flourish.

No matter how many people are along, no matter how many collective activities are planned, no matter how much the group enjoys each other's company, therefore, the final meanings of every holiday must be individual meanings. However selfish it may sound, putting the individual before the group is a necessary condition to any successful vacation. Rather than being self-centered, it means that the traveler is being self-concerned, which is fundamental to any loving relationship.

Preparing the mind for a vacation is every bit as important as preparing the body. Probably it is more important; whatever is left out here cannot be bought again at a local supermarket or souvenir stand.

CHAPTER TWO

🌺 *Knowing Who You Are*

There is an old story about a man who kept forgetting things, even where his own shoes were, and where he put his keys. Then one day he had a great idea. He decided to leave himself notes. So he wrote notes telling him where his keys were; where his shoes were; where he put his hat; where his belt was; where he left his eyeglasses, and so on and so forth. It was a long list. But after he made the list, he went to sleep with the confidence that when he awakened, nothing would be missing, and he would save time by not running around in circles, mumbling, "Where are my keys?"

Next morning, he jumped out of bed and reached for his list. He was elated. He found everything—keys, hat, eyeglasses, shoes. He even had time to do a little dance of joy. But then he stopped, puzzled. "I used to be the man who forgot everything. Now I remember where all my *things* are, but I still don't know who *I* am.

That is the question that cannot be answered by the travel brochure, the plane tickets, the itinerary, the maps, the camera, the list of restaurants, or the list of things to pack in the suitcase. The success or failure of any holiday depends on a number of variables: location, climate, companions, recreation, to name a few. But the most important single factor, far outweighing all the rest, is the character of the individual vacationer. Everything from the experiences of childhood to the adult's ability to deal with risk, challenge and the need for security combine in making up what can best be described as a person's "vacation style."

Knowing Your Origins

Each person enters adult life with a set of values and responses developed through many years of watching how others (parents, friends, teachers) manage everyday encounters and how they deal with strangers. Additional learning also comes from the social environment you are born into, from the traditions and customs passed from one generation to the next which teach you how to function within your culture.

Social heritage is as important as economic standing in establishing a personal outlook. Many ethnic groups transmit similar values from old to young regardless of individual status differences, especially, it seems, in the matter of vacation habits. For example, the child of a middle-class black family may learn that most holidays are times for "going home" to the South and the welcome of a large, extended family of cousins and grandparents and that parents will rarely go off without their children. In contrast with this tradition, the vacation memories of someone raised in a white Protestant household of the same economic level might be of going off to camp every summer and perhaps seeing his or her parents only once or twice.

Memories like these will linger into adult life, coloring later behavior. Often, whether consciously or not, we attempt to repeat the past to some degree, to recapture a memory from long ago. Thus, children who grew up in a household where holidays were looked forward to as healthy and invigorating, are more likely to expect similar rewards than are those who recall only that holidays were times for complaints about absent friends and transportation problems. If the family never took a vacation, the stage would be set for a struggle in the next generation about the need and importance of time off in their own lives. Furthermore, if the parents openly rejected the whole idea of a holiday as something frivolous and dissipating, their children may have to confront guilt, as well as habit, if they are ever to break from their past.

Another way in which a cultural inheritance can affect current vacationing is by sustaining a traveler caught in an emotional crisis. Often, at certain periods of change in one's life, going back to family origins can bring a new and necessary perspective; sometimes, seeing where you have come from will help show where you are going.

After the demise of his long but stormy marriage, a forty-two-year-old teacher of Irish descent had spent several years feeling very alone, with neither a pattern to his future nor an understanding of his past. While highly respected at school, beloved by both students and parents, he felt himself at sea, confused by the lack of purpose he saw in his life.

Then a perceptive friend, noting his confusion, suggested that he take a trip through Ireland and see the birthplace of his parents for the first time. Although he enjoyed traveling, either alone or with friends, all of his trips thus far had been to parts of the United States or to islands in the Caribbean, so he considered this advice with some trepidation. But finally he agreed, and was afterward very thankful that he had. To have experienced firsthand the culture he had sprung from stimulated a different and stronger sense of identity than he had known at work, with friends or in his former marriage. He returned feeling deeply moved and that he was beginning to lift himself from the spiritual doldrums into which he had sunk.

Knowing Your Type: The Impulsive vs. Plodding Planner

There are two distinct sorts of holiday planners, with surface differences so pronounced that they seem to be members of different species. The first is the one who merely glances up at a travel poster depicting an exciting holiday spot and within several hours has the tickets and the itinerary both firmly in hand. This person is the "impulsive" vacationer.

The second type is maddeningly deliberate in studying the alternatives. Travel folders by the score are assiduously collected, each is carefully scrutinized, underlined and ranked according to the interest they generate. Friends, relatives and travel agents are consulted, each perhaps several times. The choices are ruminated over and finally, out of what may look to the outsider like sheer exasperation, the selection is made. This sort is best described as the "plodder."

These portraits have been drawn broadly to set the type. Most vacationers fit somewhere in between, with tendencies in one direction or the other. But the capacity for being slightly impulsive or slightly deliberate, goes beyond the planning style. It often determines not only how the preparations will go, but also what the follow-through will be like.

Many of those tending toward impetuosity derive tremendous satisfaction from their ability to be spontaneous, to grasp at all the attendant excitement of dealing with the unknown. The joy that begins after a one-day deliberation on whether to safari down the Amazon is not the least bit dulled by an inconvenient three-day wait in a small village for connections or by the difficult living accommodations on the trip itself. But other impulsive sorts, having plunged headlong into the water several times only to find it freezing, are undone by their spontaneity. They select time and again holidays that are poorly suited to their real needs. What had seemed so exciting when the instant decision was first made, becomes an exercise in frustration during the actual experience.

The plodder also has ways of suffering, unique to that breed. Spending huge amounts of time in planning the trip, this traveler usually avoids obstacles, traps and mishaps commonly encountered by the impulsive vacationer. This may guarantee a hassle-free holiday, but it can also be one that is pretty much devoid of pleasure. Excitement, which is often the sum of the unknown and the unexpected, is drained by a superabundance of planning, leaving the traveler alone with anticlimax.

Before setting off for Paradise, one should be aware of his or her tendency. For this, the vacationer should answer: Are you methodical or casual in arrangements? Are you easily satisfied or quick to be disappointed? Are you grandiose in your designs? And have these traits suited you well in your previous efforts at preparation, or have they caused you endless problems in your vacation attempts?

If you notice, in reviewing past experiences, that you planned impulsively and were regularly disappointed, then for the forthcoming trip you will have to be much more reflective and deliberate during the period of preparation. You will have to spend more time on the details, considering the alternatives closely and weighing the consequences of each action. The aim is to make sure that the next time you will not find yourself stranded in the middle of surroundings totally unsuited to your needs, wondering how you ever got there.

But if you are the sort who can adapt to disappointment, who simply rolls with the punches when mishaps occur, then you can afford to be impulsive in planning your trip. You can afford to gain the benefits of the adventure that comes from dealing with the unknown since you will be set back minimally, or not at all, when suddenly faced with the unexpected.

The importance of knowing personality type before making vacation commitments cannot be overstressed. Whatever your previous experience has been, you can learn from it. Without such awareness, motive may become tangled, purpose may become confused, and the restful holiday be transformed into a maze of tension and conflict.

This situation was encountered by a family that had become enamored of camping weekends—or so they all thought—some four years previously when they were given a subscription to *Sports Afield* as a gift. After the very first trip, during which they had rented equipment, they had become so excited that they had invested in a tent, a trailer and in all the accompanying gear.

Yet after just two more of these excursions, they saw that their snap judgment had been wrong and that many conflicts arose either during or just after these trips to the wilderness. It seemed that the husband (who had led the rest of the family into its decision) was a man enthralled by roughing it, with few other people around, and with trackless forests stretching off in either direction. But his wife, who spent much of her time at home gardening and keeping house, silently regarded these trips as mere extensions of her daily routine—with the occasional added "pleasure" of cleaning fish.

Had they deliberated in advance, they might have seen this conflict before it was a problem, sparing this family a large outlay in both money and stress. The best course probably— for this couple and for most others—is to strike a careful balance between the two extremes; being impulsive about the immediate trip but being reflective and deliberate about the follow-up. This way the vacationer can retain the element of surprise, while at the same time minimize the chances for disappointment or, as sometimes, for outright despair.

Time Wise

Some people act as if they will live forever. They rarely feel rushed or pressured to complete prearranged plans; after all, if they don't get it today, there's always tomorrow. They possess what is called a *sense of timelessness* and are usually able to relax almost anywhere for many hours or days at a stretch. Others are intensely *time-aware*, acting as though each moment will be their last and if everything is not done right now, then it might never get done at all. Time must be tightly organized and structured in order to get the most out of every minute.

Although most hardly ever think about their internal time sense when vacationing, such knowledge is important. On holiday, the day can change abruptly from strict regimentation to a loose, unstructured span. An individual unable to make an internal adjustment to cope with this shift risks being unable to enjoy the experience itself.

If you feel that time is nothing but a slow-moving river (I have all the time in the world; I'll get it done *someday*), then your vacation ideas might express the same attitude. You would probably choose a loosely organized trip through several cities, or a leisurely week at the shore, or a slow, relaxing raft trip down a quiet river.

Or you may prefer planning a vacation that contrasts this take-it-as-it-comes attitude. Such an itinerary could include prearranged stopovers in a number of cities or countries with each day heavily organized and scheduled. It would be wise, however, to build in one or two "free days" for catching your breath before plunging into the whirlwind once more. The important point is to have your choice to satisfy your individual needs.

A woman described "the greatest vacation of my life" at a Midwest ski resort, praising the totally "unstructured, unhurried, free and timeless" atmosphere she found. Since this was an individual who led a highly ordered life the rest of the year, her description was surprising. Exploring the experience at greater length, a pattern emerged that put the holiday into greater perspective. Each day she awoke at the same time, had breakfast with her husband, joined a ski class for a six-hour lesson (including lunch), stopped off at one of the cafes near the slopes, joined her husband for dinner in town before returning to the lodge for an hour of bridge and then slept until the break of another (identical) day.

Unwittingly, this woman managed to fulfill her stated "need" for unordered adventure in the very same setting that met her covert desire for order and predictability. This wonderful "accident" cannot be anticipated by everyone. There is no substitute for conscious self-understanding.

Role Reversal?

Just as you can switch time clocks on vacations, there is also the opportunity to change life-styles. The longing for familiarity which keeps many from venturing very far from their environment can inhibit flexibility. People generally tend to cluster about with others most like themselves. Singles will seek out and spend most of their time with other singles, childless couples with other childless couples and large families with other large families. Yet the chance to change a habitual role is available on holiday as perhaps nowhere else. It is a chance that can offer unexpected rewards if only one will take the risk.

These rewards are illustrated in the experience told by a childless couple who had arranged to join six other families on a camping weekend in the Blue Ridge Mountains. While they had all known one another for several years, these two were seriously concerned about their ability to handle several days with such a wide assortment of children ranging in age from infancy to early adolescence.

No sooner had the trip begun, however, than they began experiencing the warm feelings they had felt long ago in their own extended families, with the two of them this time assuming the roles of deeply cherished but rarely seen aunt and uncle. The children were fascinated with stories of the past and of unfamiliar places; even the adults enjoyed having them around as a respite from lives spent only with others very much like themselves. And for the couple, the weekend was an opportunity to experience life as others lived it, to share in unfamiliar feelings and to be exposed to different attitudes.

Role change on a vacation can be an opportunity for all concerned. A harried businessman can become the cook on a camping trip; a housewife can become the business agent and organizer on a multi-city tour; a young single person can become a helping aunt or uncle at a family resort. The variations are almost endless and so are the rewards.

Knowing Each Other

Both before and during a trip, consideration of the needs of a companion or other members of a holiday group is essential to a successful vacation. Yet all too often, travelers behave as though they are all alone, with no one to look out for beyond themselves, with no interests beyond their own. Unfortunately, it is never that easy.

After seeing a movie about the islands, a middle-aged couple decided to spend their holiday in Hawaii for what they *assumed* were similar reasons. They did not bother to communicate their reactions to the film, and supposed that the other had been impressed by the same things. So, with no discussion, the reservations were made, the bags were packed and the two started off for Honolulu.

The wife saw in this trip an opportunity to "turn on" her unexciting and overworked husband by exposing him to sexually stimulating surroundings. Because she had not shared these expectations with him—having just assumed—she could not have suspected that he, too, had needs and desires, but that they were totally different than her own.

Anthropology was his hobby, and he saw in the coming adventure a wonderful chance to study a land with a multi-national heritage dating back to the very beginnings of civilization. So while his wife envisioned scenes of seduction beneath every waving palm, he imagined himself as Margaret Mead.

The first two days—with the time change, the jet lag and settling into their new surroundings—passed calmly; both of them were too exhausted for it to be otherwise. But finally, on the third evening, the wife made her move appearing before dinner in a sheer, sexy nightgown, ready for several languorous hours of love-making before a romantic, late supper in their room. Her husband exploded. Calling her display "lewd" and "indecent," he stormed from the room and was absent for several hours, leaving her with her frustrated fantasies, shattered by his rejection.

The lesson here is that sharing expectations, both in advance and during the vacation itself, can often make the vital difference between success and failure on any holiday. This does not mean that every member of every family will be totally gratified with every vacation. Such a blissful circumstance is impossible. But if everyone is encouraged to express individual wishes and concerns before the trip, then there definitely will be less chance for unpleasant surprise during the trip and less potential for irritation as well.

Understanding the Life Cycle

When determining the likely course of a holiday, it is important to consider the vacationer's age and station in life. Such observers as Erik Erikson, Roger Gould and Gail Sheehy, writing of the effects of age on behavior, have all

THE LIFE-CYCLE AND VACATION CHARACTERISTICS

AGE	CYCLE CHARACTERISTICS	VACATION CHARACTERISTICS
18–22	Break from parents Heavy peer involvement "Life is just around the corner"	Being with peers Activity is less important than who one shares it with
23–28	Establishing autonomy Living is "now"	Excitement, pleasure Companions less important than how well time is spent
29–34	Questioning self—is this the best way to be Identifying with children but maintaining some separation from them	Vacation extremely important and significant in one's life Much scrutiny and criticism of activities Conflict over spending time with children vs. other adults
35–43	Much introspection, questioning values, life Finiteness of life and urgency of time "One last chance to make it big" Thoughts of changes in marriage, social life, business	Much emphasis on having "meaningful" vacations Exercising of fantasies not capable of expressions in daily life Increasing cultural pursuits

AGE	CYCLE CHARACTERISTICS	VACATION CHARACTERISTICS
44–58	Resignation and relief about finiteness of time; "the die is cast"	Increased criticism of experiences and sensitivity to rejection
	Decreased emphasis on friends	Vacations should be comfortable and familiar
	Increased dependence on one other person	Continuing cultural pursuits, beginning returns to "homeland"
	Greater competition and criticism of others	
59 and beyond	Mellowing and warming to others; decreased negativism	Increased involvement with others on vacation
	Spouse and friends seen as valued companions	Vacations taken with more meaning for one's life—homeland returns, cultural pursuits
	Time sense is "now," future less important	Heightened enjoyment of experience
	Consolidating meaningfulness of one's life and contributions	
	Hunger for relations with others	

pointed out that there are certain characteristics which tend to appear in people of roughly the same age and which influence both emotional outlook and behavior. These traits tend to make people at the same point in their lives think and feel in ways that are generally similar and predictable. These influences should be considered when contemplating current activities and, more important, when imagining future direction.

This is *not* to say that everyone is locked into certain feelings or into having only certain interests at certain ages. Not everyone comes from the same mold. Most are uniquely shaped by a variety of influences. But what *is* true is that specific stages in the life cycle will affect interests and behavior as much as socioeconomic, racial or ethnic position.

The chart* on pages 18–19 describes those characteristics common to most people during each stage of the life cycle. A projection of how these tendencies might show themselves as vacation desires has been added at the different points. It must be remembered, though, that *nothing*—not age, sex, marital condition, or anything else—locks a person into a set course. Nor are the age brackets inviolate; if a person at forty-five enjoys behavior indicated for someone twenty years younger, there is no cause for alarm.

These are simply guidelines, suggestions of a pattern that researchers have observed working in most people. They are not goals to aim for, but merely indications of widespread tendencies.

A vacation is an investment in one's self and in one's rela-

* Adapted from Gould, Roger L., "*The Phases of Adult Life:* A Study in Developmental Psychology," *American Journal of Psychiatry,* 129:5, November 1972.

tionships. Since knowing yourself gives you better tools for making decisions about how best to enjoy the holiday, an understanding of your position in the life cycle can help protect that investment.

CHAPTER THREE

❧ The Experience

Each person's experience of a vacation is affected by any one or all of the traits discussed in the last chapter. These traits form the individual's unique personality. Vacation types also have unique "personalities." Whether it be a "Rest and Relaxation" week at the summer house or a "Culture Quest" to Turkey—each type of vacation has its own basic characteristics. In other words, before putting down the first payment, a traveler should consider not only his or her own temperament but also the intrinsic style of the vacation selected. As some people are impetuous or spontaneous, so others are more regimented or scheduled. Their vacation needs are entirely different. What is important is for you to appreciate these varieties of experience and to harmonize and counterpoint your own habits, desires and needs with them.

The following varieties of the vacation experience are not intended to suggest that every vacation should be restricted to one of these types, or that all holidays ought to be more of one sort than another or, especially, that any one occurs only in isolation from any other. If people take a few days off to rest and do nothing special in the middle of a two-week ski vacation, or if they shop for souvenirs while tracking down the birthplace of ancestors, then they are really responding simultaneously to different needs or desires. The following sections break it all down: first identifying each type individually and then considering some of its implications. It is up to the traveler to make his or her own combinations.

No one will be attracted to all varieties of vacation experiences at any one time. Each person, depending on age, personality and many other factors has different needs and desires. Yet no one should automatically discount the possibility to realize new opportunities. Experience is like a fertile field. Overplanting in any one crop exhausts the soil; but if the planting is balanced, alternated with the seasons and sufficiently rotated, then the soil will be productive, constantly renewed and enriched. Although no one can (or can *want* to) attempt everything described here in the same holiday, the richest individual is the one who can draw from these vacation types freely.

Self-improvement

Few vacations are as gratifying as those devoted to self-improvement. An increasing number of Americans have made the condition of their bodies a major concern. Municipal tennis courts used to stand empty most of the time—except for the kids using them for basketball practice. Now they have become so overcrowded and overused that many communities have resorted to long sign-in sheets and permits to bring some order to the masses of would-be players hoping for an hour to improve their stamina and their skills.

It even seems possible that the traditional image of American men grouped around TV sets watching football games every weekend might someday give way to the sight of both sexes spending the day on the tennis courts. Already, the trend from spectator to participant shows some signs of endurance. The recreation and sporting goods industry, for an obvious example, is one of the largest and fastest growing in the country, and there are shelves of books on everything from improving your golf game to becoming a better cross-country skier.

Nor has the mind been left far behind the body in the quest for self-improvement. The encounter weekends, sensitivity training retreats, art, film and Shakespeare seminars have all given to many a sense of having expanded their emotional range or broadened their intellectual horizons.

This increase in both interest and participation in all possible areas of self-improvement has naturally spilled over into using vacation and leisure time to polish and perfect these interests.

People are discovering that a well-structured and organized week or two devoted to tennis, skiing or even weight reducing, if handled properly, can be one of the most rewarding and truly satisfying experiences of the year. Moreover, it can satisfy in ways that are individually valuable and not the result of social pressures or conditioning. Yet the "if handled properly" caution must be added, since there are some potential pitfalls and dangers in undertaking one of these vacations.

For most people, athletic activities are gratifying psychologically because they appeal to the almost universal need to feel good physically. They allow one to participate in a process that affords rapid gratification resulting from concrete effort. Rarely is it possible to grasp the rewards so immediately. Rarely is the entire process of effort and gratification made so clear and straightforward.

Since self-improvement camps are usually highly involving and exhausting, both physically and emotionally, the vacationer-student can come away from the end of each day with a feeling of having really tried, of having given as much as possible and of still being happy—even if the sport is not yet mastered, the weight is not yet lost or the problems are not yet solved, at least not that day. There was, after all, the honest attempt, and there is probably nothing that is quite so gratifying as being able to say truthfully, "I really tried. I gave it all I could."

Another asset to this type of vacation, a more hidden asset, is its high degree of structure. At a tennis camp, for example, there is a predetermined and prearranged schedule for each day. Even the evenings are structured, since that is the time when people get together for a review of the day, to rehash their experiences with a view toward a brighter tomorrow.

Little is left to chance at such places, and the problem of what to do about the unexpected, how to deal with the unplanned, is obviated—it just never comes up. For many people, the meaning of these weeks is that the great weight that has been pressing down all year is (briefly) lifted. Their sense of relief is almost palpable.

Few vacationers returning from one of these back-to-school experiences is ever very disappointed. Yet, because not everyone can be wholly satisfied all of the time, because not everyone is happy doing what everyone else is happy doing, there is, inevitably, some discontent. There are those, for example, who should never have attempted one of these self-improvement vacations in the first place.

Someone leading a rigid, highly regimented life may be more in need of a holiday with much less structure even though feeling slightly uncomfortable at even the thought of being somewhere without organization. Possibly, such a person should look for a vacation in which the boundaries are less defined than in a formal self-improvement setting—tennis or skiing without the rigid demands of daily instruction, for instance.

Another who might consider avoiding situations of this sort —at least for the time being—is that individual who has just suffered through a particularly deflating personal experience and whose self-esteem is at a low ebb; who feels "one more failure and I've had it." But no inflexible rules can be applied. A self-improvement vacation that makes few demands and is only mildly challenging at this point, can prove just the thing for helping to close the wounds and improve self-confidence.

The decision must be an individual one based on a review of your recent experience and knowledge of your personal vacation style. How you have been feeling prior to the holiday, how regulated your day-to-day activities are and your ability to tolerate a lot of structure on a vacation all must be considered. So must your need for freedom from scheduling and, most of all, your ability to weave your own needs into the fabric of the vacation.

This last point is essential. A self-improvement vacation is still a vacation: a time to recover your energies, a time to follow your own desires. If your holiday begins to look just like your work week, then watch out, for that kind of "improvement" cannot be for the self.

Rest and Relaxation

Often there is the daydream: "Wouldn't it be perfect just to take a week off and do nothing but relax?" This common fantasy of days spent in a hammock somewhere gently rocking away cares and responsibilities, or else of long hours reading those special books reserved for such times or just soaking up the sun is one we all share from time to time.

It is also one few of us will ever take advantage of in such an absolute way. Not many people can remain in a state of continuous relaxation for long without some kind of planned activity to reduce the "weight" of just doing nothing. And so there are always plenty of options, lots of things to do, lots of ways to keep busy, a legion of planned activities that spare us the challenge of being left with nothing but ourselves. Although the *idea* of a holiday "just to relax" is perhaps the easiest of all to come up with and is, in many ways, the most appealing, it is at the same time a most difficult idea to sustain.

Then why bother fantasizing about rest and relaxation if it is such a problem? Why go through all the trouble of constructing an impossibility? The answer is that it is a very real need within everyone. It enables a person to hear the voice of the inner self with a special clarity. Most of one's life is spent

responding to the needs of others, to the imposed scheduling
of the work day, the school day, the demands of children or
the demands of community membership. But after all these
calls are answered, there is little time left to just relax. And
somehow, people may forget exactly how to do it. Eventually
some will even become anxious at the mere thought of being
alone—afraid that there may be nothing to do.

At times this uneasiness about being left alone with the self
can lead to actual feelings of guilt about any form of relaxation. It may lead to the declaration that "I shouldn't be resting;
I should be doing something constructive with my time—
working, mowing the lawn, washing the dishes, something,
anything." This scolding inner voice can make us feel that we
are wasting time if not forever engaged in some profitable activity.

But, it is a person's birthright to have some moments alone,
to play, to relax, to rest. *Doing nothing is an integral part of
self-renewal*, it provides the breathing space needed by everyone to get oriented and organized, to sort out plans and to
rehearse for the future. There comes a point at which you
have gone far enough—have done enough things—and that is
the point at which relaxation becomes essential.

Therefore, on all types of vacations a time of recuperation
should be an important element of a well-planned holiday. In
between the sight-seeing, the scuba diving, the dining out,
there should be some moments set aside for unwinding and ab-
sorbing.

But what of the vacationers who decide to make relaxation
the central theme of the holiday rather than just an integrated
side issue? Must they commit themselves to ten days of total
inactivity? Should every moment be of Nirvana-like bliss? Ac-

tually, this kind of holiday is probably best achieved without
any rigid expectations. It helps to have a back-up plan in re-
serve just in case of sudden "relaxation weariness." When those
structures that are natural parts of the rest of one's life begin
to protest their exclusion, and when that protest becomes too
loud there should be some way to relieve the noise. The idea
of a vacation built around just reading or lying on the beach
soaking up the sun can easily become every bit as constraining
as the structure someone is trying to forget. For this reason,
there must be alternatives.

If a woman is on the beach alone with her picnic lunch and
the latest Vonnegut novel (just as she had dreamed when she
first planned this holiday), and she begins to feel lonely, she
has two options. One is to force herself into remaining there
until sunburned and until she has gotten through the planned
number of chapters. The second is to recognize and to act on
her desire to be with people. The right choice here is obvious.
This vacation is hers alone; she need not measure up to any
preconceived standards of relaxing on the beach. When a
vacationer is stranded on an artificial image (the woman forc-
ing herself to remain on the beach until tanned despite her real
desires), she denies herself the flexibility and the chance for
variety that is so essentially human.

The key to success on such a holiday is listening to your
personal needs and answering them while at the same time
providing yourself the opportunity for easing out of the main-
stream and into repose. Real relaxation is a goal reached only
through a layered process, a careful stripping away of all the
levels of surface activity. It comes only at the end of a lengthy
procedure involving a step-by-step elimination of tension and
worry. First, a person must stop running: physically, emo-

tionally, mentally. This, the tier lying closest to the surface, is the easiest for most people to understand and the one few will bother to go beyond. But this is only the first step. Next, and far more difficult, feelings of guilt about just wasting time must be resolved. This is the barrier between most people and real relaxation. Then third, once that obstruction has been overcome, a tolerance of fantasy and play has to be established. Finally, there comes the reward: The individual who perseveres in relaxation and in concentration will gain, even if only momentarily, a serene state of being in which inner and outer events are fully audible and visible, unmixed with anxiety.

Suppose we visualize the course of this evolution in terms of the woman on the beach. She returns the following day with her blanket but without her book, uncertain of how long she will stay. At first, she is just uncomfortable: wishing she had a soda, feeling each grain of sand on the blanket chafing against her skin, thinking about all the work left behind at the office. The sound of pounding typewriters within her head grows louder than the surf, and she can't get the job out of her mind.

But gradually she senses that her thoughts are settling: her work is farther away now and it will take care of itself and she should not worry. Slowly, the busy obsessions which plague her fade, and she becomes aware, most of all, that the sand is warm. Feelings of drowsiness and heat have not penetrated very far into her body, however, before she begins to remember how her father used to yell at her if she were just to stretch out on the grass and try to sun herself while he was mowing the lawn. And how he then would make her rake up the clippings.

Now she hears seagulls squawk, and the memory of her fa-

ther, of his anger, melts away. She feels a peaceful content-
ment till another reverie begins. She recalls the recent breakup
with a man she has been dating. The memory makes her feel
sad and alone. She shifts her position uncomfortably.

But then she is startled by the surf licking at her foot. With
the incoming tide, she is drawn gently into the present. Her
thoughts cease and she is no longer drawn toward the past.
The blue of the sky is blazing through her, and she can inhale
the breeze, taste its salt, feel its tang. Breathing evenly and
freely—for what feels like the first time in months—she takes
it all in: those incomparable gifts of the sun, of the waves, of
the sand. Now she is relaxing.

Rest and relaxation have opened this woman to a particularly subtle form of play. Just as sports and games are recreation for the body, so relaxation and the aimless play of the
senses, are recreation for the mind. The importance of this
sort of mind-play to any individual is hard to exaggerate, for
without it a potential of experience is forever lost.

The road into that state, as the illustration demonstrates,
first passes through levels of tension and control to encounter
the fears and memories of the past, until the buried repository
of true contemplation and aesthetic vision is able to emerge
uncluttered at last.

This process allows us to discover that there are really several bodies lying within each body, nesting inside one another
like Chinese boxes. The outer boxes are mechanized and highly
defended (even against their owners) so they might successfully operate in a highly structured and social world. The
inner boxes are those of receptivity and play, those lying beyond reason and designed to emerge in moments of complete

security. Moments that can be reached at times of total relaxation.

Roughing It

Why do people pack gear into station wagons and drive down dusty roads for miles just for the pleasure of pitching a balky tent in the wind and rain? Why do they tote packs and trudge up steep, zigzag trails just to sleep on the cold, damp ground by a sputtering campfire? Why do campers by the thousands lie beside lakes in Central Michigan, along the rivers of Washington and of Upstate New York looking at the summer stars, listening to the unfamiliar sounds of the wilderness night, scratching at their mosquito bites and their poison ivy or nursing their cuts and bruises.

Many of them have left their air-conditioners and their dishwashers, their designer clothing, their accountants, lawyers and paperwork behind. In return, they have found that relaxation—which can be so difficult in their own home—is a natural accompaniment to roughing it in the wild. This exchange is why they go.

They have also discovered that hiking, riding or just pitching camp leads to a complete sort of exhaustion that is basic to real relaxation. It is distinct from mental tiredness, which is often accompanied by tensions, agitation and even sleepless nights. The physical exhaustion of camping, because there is little conscious thought behind it, liberates the mind and provides the foundation for that pleasant kind of reverie that leaves a person unmindful of the passage of hours. Many who rough it are answering the call for breathing space and for a more deliberate rhythm; they are answering the call, in other words, for a time of renewal.

There are other assets to roughing it. There is more opportunity to recover the feeling of shared experience and of
comradeship in encountering the raw elements of nature with
others. Whether rafting down the rapids with a group of
companions, training with a team of fellow climbers for an as-
sault on Mount Rainier, hunting with friends in Tennessee or
simply camping with the family, new bonds of human relat-
edness emerge. Or rather, the old bonds—the primitive connections between people—are rediscovered. When working as
part of a group united for a common purpose, the individual
becomes one with that group. Each must rely on one another
to gather wood for the fire, to go down to the river for water,
to pitch or to fold the tent.

For many people, surrounded daily with "cold concept and
design," the sight of a tree only triggers a mental notation of
the word rather than a feeling for the thing itself. Roughing it
reclaims the feelings and allows the sensuous moments; it permits one to touch some important essence hidden below our
daily experience. Campers, hikers, climbers and every sort of
nature person knows those moments of poetry, of what the
English Romantics of the nineteenth century called, simply
and perfectly, "the Sublime." These are the times when all
surroundings seem to gain a new clarity, a refreshed perspective; when single leaves become visible and their form becomes important, or when the break of a bird rustling up from
a bush becomes as audible as the crash of a cymbal. In such
moments, the individual alone in the forest is not really alone
at all but is part of the larger family of all living things. People
rough it for revelations of this kind.

Of course, all is not a pure experience of epiphany and communion. There are also the status fights over campground position, the grumbling over assigned chores, about who left

what at home, even about those details of the costume drama
that have penetrated into the deepest part of the forest. Hats
of Irish wool, multibladed Swiss army knives, leather carrying
cases, bamboo fly rods and down sleeping bags all are part of
the cherished baggage of the "compleat camper." But this display of possessions, at least, can be much more peripheral when
we rough it. Sometimes, in fact, it is nearly reversed.

There is an appeal everyone remembers from childhood of
playing in the dirt and splashing through the puddles, of getting all grubby and not caring how you look. Camping out
satisfies those happy—and long suppressed—feelings. Suddenly
not having to shave, shower or comb your hair for a few days
—smelling sweaty and feeling earthy—can be liberating for
many men or women. For a week, ten days or a month, the
camper is beyond the cosmetic advertisements, beyond a social
sense of chic.

For some, roughing it means a return to the first hunting or
fishing trip with father. For others, it is a way to "prove"
themselves physically, to show that they can take a pounding
and still get up, or to remember their careers as Scouts. Perhaps because of the directness and simplicity of insight in the
wild, or that life seems easier and less cluttered, a great many
childhood memories seem to return during encounters with
nature. To many people, the trail through the woods also becomes like a half-known, badly understood inner search for an
important memory of the past.

Some people harbor a secret suspicion that civilization is a
veneer and that someday they may be called upon to be rough
and hardy, just like their forefathers. This doubt about the
permanence of mechanized lives is about as close as most ever
get to challenging the reality of the factory or the office, the

dishwasher or the TV. So instead, these modern pioneers meet
the challenge by shedding the sophistication and returning to
that animal body that is the basis of all a person can ever know
or do. Their answer to these doubts about civilization is to
"rough it."

A Royal Week (or Two)   2008814

Many people view their vacation as synonymous with luxu-
rious escape, a time of insulation from work and from the
other pressures of ordinary routine. It is a time for the wishes
and dreams that have sustained the individual through long
months on the job to be translated at last into a starlit reality.

A man who commutes to Chicago through the long months
of winter blizzards may imagine a golf course set by the side
of a shimmering pool and a tennis court—and all of it but a
few steps from his hotel room. His wife, on the other hand,
might fancy a solid week without the demands of their children, without the telephone ringing, without the supermarket
hassle and without her part-time job selling encyclopedias. Together, they dream of a time when they can be alone at last,
without all the distractions of home, when they can take long,
lonely walks as they did when they were courting, when they
can dance together, when they can meet new people. In their
struggle to raise a family, they have found themselves fre-
quently busy, evening after evening, without even a moment
to be alone with each other. Now they vow to make their an-
nual vacation an experience of genuine satisfaction and a
fulfillment of their grandest wishes for being special people.

Because this couple, like so many others, spend much of
their time devoted to the needs of others, on their vacation

they want others to take care of them for a change, they want
to set their own limits for once. So they are interested only in
the very best service, right from the time they get in the taxi
for the ride to the airport to the time they return home. They
feel it is worth paying extra to avoid unnecessary wrinkles in
their plans. They want an ocean view and will pay to get it.
They want fine stores to shop in and will go to a resort fa-
mous for its exclusive boutiques. They want steak and lobster
every night and are willing to pay the price for the very best.
Since they are both conscious that this vacation is for them
and for their needs, they refuse to cut corners or skimp on the
extras. He jokes that "nothing is too good for the working
class." She smiles as she answers that no one has less leisure
time than the working housewife and mother.

The success of their holiday depends on this kind of banter-
ing mood as well as on extensive preparations. Yet, since it is
intended as an extended celebration of all the things they most
love to do, our King and Queen cannot sit passively on the
sidelines expecting others to know by instinct exactly what
they want at every minute. They must plan out the adventure
well ahead of time, testing different travel agents and various
options. Many other choices must also be made in advance,
from the obvious ones about location and the duration of their
stay to whether or not to travel with friends or how to divide
the time among the various forms of recreation. The most important thing for our regal pair to know beforehand is that the
particular resort they have settled on offers a combination of
activities that is responsive to them and to their personal needs
with an absolute minimum of friction.

As with any plan, the regal holiday can go wrong at any
time. Nobody controls the weather, illness, strikes by the hotel

staff or the innumerable other uncertainties that can afflict any vacationer. The only protection here is a flexible attitude that meets all experience, whatever its nature, with a determination to roll with those waves that cannot be controlled while waiting for the perfect crest.

If you select such a holiday, don't be surprised if a friend who feels that vacations are meant for climbing across the pyramids of Egypt or the ruins of Greece looks with disapproval at your decision. Remember, your desire for a pampered time does not mean you are withdrawing from life or rehearsing for retirement. This vacation will be filled with the good things of life—golfing, swimming, meeting new people, shopping, sight-seeing, sampling the local night life and the best restaurants. Wanting nothing to come between you and your desires—no lines for the golf course, no screaming children around the pool—is not bad. In fact, tasting the fruit of your labor—perhaps even satisfying those touches of envy when your budget meant a take-out Chinese dinner for six instead of supper for two by candlelight—is your prerogative. Everyone deserves two weeks to feel like the most important people in the world.

The Culture Quest

Some people will be students forever. They will spend their vacations learning about how the past connects with the present, or how the paintings and sculpture of a certain period reflect the social conditions of that time, or how ancient dreams grew into modern realities. Their search might take them through the labyrinth of the Roman catacombs, the Mayan pyramids of Guatemala or the colonial towns of Vir-

ginia. In return for this concern, the world will take on new
dimensions, setting the demands of the contemporary pace
against the traditions and values of other cultures. The process
of learning is a gyroscopic one, constantly measuring one
world against another, maintaining a delicate equilibrium between the two.

For those who want their learning organized, there are
numerous excursions sponsored by museums and specialty tour
groups. These are designed to present an interrelated picture
of a region, from its art to its culture to its traditions. On a
more formally academic level, many American universities
provide educational/vacation programs during the summers.
These one- or two-week seminars, on subjects ranging from
the plays of Shakespeare to mountain folk culture, include
low-cost dormitory living, social gatherings with fellow students and the use of campus recreational facilities. Being
learners by nature, culture seekers may find such vacations
close to perfect. They provide guided access to backstage
viewing and a deeper understanding of what went into the
making of a certain artifact, or a historical event or how the
present was produced by the forces of the past.

But cultural discoveries are not restricted to such formal set-
tings alone, nor are they limited only to the dedicated "stu-
dent." There are times when many people feel that they are
becoming disconnected from something important, an attachment that may be physical, emotional or social. During such
periods, their sense of wholeness—that unique blend of inner
and outer circumstances and forces—is somehow put out of
balance, and a person questions his or her most basic routines
or highest ideals. Here is where the quest for culture—the re-
generating of old connections or the discovery of new ones—
can be especially helpful.

An active feminist recently returned from a trip to Greece and expressed her own moment of inspiration which came during a visit to the Parthenon. There was a short layover in Athens before making connections for the Aegean Islands and arrival in the city triggered an unexpected desire to redefine some earlier feelings and to re-examine her past. (Since her awestruck undergraduate philosophy days at the University of Michigan, she had developed ambivalent feelings toward the ancient Greeks and the cultural traditions they inspired.)

After checking into the hotel, she took a cab to the Plaka and walked toward the steep stone steps leading up to the Acropolis. From there she could see down to the great theater of Dionysos with the city stretching out beyond. As she continued looking at the ancient spectacle and thinking over her life she grew conscious of some sort of ritual going on within her. She was not just sight-seeing and putting items in her cultural shopping bag, but was really measuring herself against the surroundings. She was comparing her position to that of the successive builders of the Parthenon and to the world they represented. She was redefining her relationship with the forces of a culture she had been taught in college to hold in such wonder. Now, at forty, she understood that she was no longer overwhelmed by this patriarchal culture, nor did she want to attack or reject it. Instead, she was able to appreciate the expressions of the ideals she saw around her while at the same time feel confidence in her own position of independence and self-reliance.

This is the real landscape of culture, full of personal meanings. It not only speaks to a person out of the past but also allows that person to speak for himself or herself, to experience the present.

Wherever people go, their personal connection to the arti-
facts of the culture (their sense of culture) is what contributes
to their feeling of belonging, of participating in the making
of the world. Whether they visit the Alamo, the Lincoln Me-
morial or the Buddhist shrines of Sri Lanka, they are able to
participate in the ideals and dreams of a heritage that is both
ancient and contemporary. The cultural vacation brings satisfaction through the affinity it gives the traveler for the politi-
cal leaders, the log cabin builders, the artists—for all of the
makers and all of the joiners who have constructed our world
out of the elements given them by the past.

The Status Quest

Status-consciousness is the "price" people must pay for having been born social animals. It is a necessary condition for all
human relationships and it is basic to all human behavior. Everyone, regardless of occupation, standing or income, has a
necessary—and healthy—concern for position.

Unfortunately, a person's status is never a constant, but
varies widely from group to group, and even from time to
time. On vacations, this can be particularly difficult. Some
people feel insulted if a travel agent even suggests a tour of the
South Pacific or a cruise to Alaska just because "everyone" is
going this year. For them, it must be the tiny resort in the
Dominican Republic or an unknown ski area in northern
Maine. Their status rewards come from the vacation discoveries they make. Others, to whom familiar companions and
familiar social situations are important, are happiest when
lying on the sands of Waikiki or when skiing in Colorado—
along with thousands of others.

Similarly, what is rewarding to one group may pass by another completely unacknowledged. A man who takes his friends out for a week of fishing in his private boat will find immediate gratification in the shared pleasure they will experience. On the other hand, someone traveling alone, buying Indian jewelery in Guatemala, finds the most satisfaction only upon returning home where others can appreciate these purchases.

Wherever the vacation and whatever the conditions, it is essential to remember that no one can gain status from all groups all the time. A woman might be especially proud of her solo camera safari through Kenya—only to be told by her family that she was crazy to have gone. At the same time her consciousness-raising group will glorify her for her independence, her fellow teachers might attack her for being absent at an important faculty meeting, while her students will simply be in awe of her. This woman's standing differs in all these outside groups.

Approval from *somewhere* is fundamental to the human condition. But, since position and role vary so widely from person to person, a degree of "status insecurity"—the fear of doing the wrong thing for the wrong audience—is also inescapable. Vacationers, being in a situation of inevitable fluctuation, are susceptible to this condition.

Possibly the most intense sort of status insecurity awaiting holiday travelers is that produced by arriving at an unfamiliar elegant resort a complete outsider. It is frightening to appear at a cocktail party given for the new guests to meet each other. Even the most jaded holiday veteran may feel a tightness in the stomach. Are you dressed appropriately? Will the others speak more languages? Have they been to more places? In some of the more formal vacation spots, this ritual can assume truly intimidating dimensions, with many people gathered around the perimeter of the room, cringing behind their drinks, convinced that all the rest have known one another for years. This is the time when doubts will be magnified, fears will be let loose and status insecurity will rise to the surface.

A few resorts, such as those of the Club Mediterranee, make a conscious effort to reduce this sort of anxiety and concern by stripping layers off people—by presenting them in sandals and bathing suits—and by enforcing an informal rule that occupations are of no interest to anyone. Conversations purposely focus on the present.

Such vacations force people to operate from a slender range of conversational options. They are ideally suited both to those who are at all doubtful of their social role, and to those who are always tied to their professions, forever "the doctor," "the teacher," "the judge." It is refreshing for many of these people *not* to be asked what one does or where one lives for a change and instead to focus exclusively on the present moment.

Sometimes, however, those who have the "highest" social standing are the ones who find it easiest to surrender their status. Others are very often feeling uncertainty about their position in life and are fearful of even the briefest renouncing of a hard-won position.

Another group, those who feel "status deprived" in their daily lives, can improve these feelings by remedying distortions about themselves. The best way is to broaden contacts outside the family, the firm, the neighborhood, even outside the whole local "scene." Vacations can prove extremely helpful in doing this. Chance encounters in dining rooms, on tennis courts, in museums and elsewhere can lead to lasting friendships and new business associations. Or they may just give one a better feeling about himself or herself and a clearer idea about how others live. The more real "experience" about different people you have, the less your envy will be and the more you can appreciate the essential humanness in all of us.

Seeking Sex

Brief sexual encounters are full of potential for satisfaction. They are intense but limited, allowing the participants to be at their best all the time. The suspense of the first meeting, the surprise and excitement of a sudden erotic attraction, the security of a total mutual exploration of bodies, feelings, lives and the ecstatic abandonment to passion—all of these might occur in the space of a single week.

Hoping for such pleasures, a single woman travels to a "swinging" resort in search of romantic adventure, a husband declares to his wife that they are going off to Florida on a second honeymoon, a gay male joins a homosexual vacation tour to the Caribbean. All of them are filled with the anticipation of intimate relationships and immediate rewards. Before you go, however, it is important that you understand the terms of the adventure.

Single people, for instance, tend to fall into one of two categories. Either they will be playing a full-scale courting game, or else they will be hoping for a passing relationship that will prove temporarily satisfying to their needs. In the former case, they are searching for an intimate companion, sexual partner, and perhaps ultimately a co-parent. For both cases, a successful hunt can best be pursued in places that most reflect their *own* real interests. There is a fundamental difference between looking for a companion who loves the outdoors at a "singles only" ranch in Wyoming and carrying the same search into a Los Angeles bar at three in the morning.

It also helps to keep in mind that this vacation (as any vacation) belongs to you alone, whether you make the match of your life or not. If a friend met her husband at a tennis camp and your only experience with the sport was during gym class six years ago, then be careful. Do not imagine that the same tennis camp will automatically produce the same results for you. Not only may you not meet someone special, but you may find out that tennis is just not your cup of tea.

But let's say that you love sailing and decide to go on a windjammer cruise. This time, because you are already satisfying your own desires, a romantic affair will be an extra dividend instead of an essential demand. Since it is only a short, predefined time, and since the holiday will not succeed or fail solely on the basis of a passing relationship, you may feel no need to hold back. If you do what you like, there is no need to fear being swallowed by the other person's interests. Even if the affair turns sour, there is still the adventure of being under full sail.

The physical limits to such a situation also suggest the necessary caution: An affair with no strings attached is only that, and neither partner should enter into it by investing his personal self-esteem toward making a lasting attachment. A person is not merely a sexual object. While, obviously, the enjoyment of such an interlude cannot be restricted to sex alone, expectations must be carefully tailored to the short time of intense togetherness. If the relationship happens to endure, then it will do so on its own terms and in its own time.

For married couples or long-time companions, a different approach to an intimate vacation is called for—one that has room for changing of familiar behavior. A holiday for this couple is an opportunity to break from routine, and it can reawaken emotions of sexual attraction and arousal that once existed. But old habits are strong. If certain conflicts are still unresolved or if they have been submerged, they can stand in the way of pleasure.

The best plan is to delay. A wise couple takes time and trusts time. Time to settle in. Time to enjoy experiences like dancing and swimming together. Time to share plans for the future. Their non-compulsive, rhythmic tolerance is very different from avoiding sex; it is accumulating a reservoir of positive feelings about one another and about their surroundings that will later lead them into rich and harmonious love-making.

Part of this slow preparation is an apology for past insults and misdeeds. Good love-making is not so much a matter of virtuoso bedroom technique as it is of simple understanding that the strain of normal living may interfere with pleasure. Honest concern for this pain is an essential part of the preparation for sharing positive emotions. People must learn to deal with their resentments and disputes before they can hope for anything better.

In all cases, sexual fulfillment on vacation depends mainly on an awareness of personal emotional needs. The voluntary letting go of all inhibitions for a plunge into the rip tide of sexual passion can be an unbalancing and even frightening experience. Anxieties about performance or success can be shared. Humor and tolerance are crucial for sexual security between two people. The quest for sexual satisfaction cannot be one's primary interest on a vacation and should not override the quest for personal satisfaction. You are a "self" and not simply a "sex organ."

Where the Bargains Are

Some people love to shop. No matter where they happen to be—at a huge department store, a tiny grocery, a jewelry shop, even at the local supermarket—shopping transports them to a sensual "banquet." To them, the opportunity to vacation *means* the opportunity to shop: exploring back-alley markets, spending savings in a spree, discovering bargains, collecting goods, souvenirs and gifts to bring home by the trunkful.

Shopping like this is fundamentally different from buying at home. It is not for survival or for necessities alone; it is *playing* with needs rather than merely satisfying them. It is expanding and exploring beyond the basic requirements of food, dress and furnishing. It is, in other words, crossing into the area of sport.

The direct contact of giving personally to strangers the fruit of one's work and receiving in exchange their products, enhances the game. When buying is a face-to-face transaction instead of one mediated by the salesperson at the sleek new shopping mall, many feel a primitive satisfaction in directly bartering for their desires. In such circumstances, they may even tolerate overpaying or buying something they don't really need. Reason and logic are secondary. Strange, shieldlike objects will be carted home from Turkey (where they only cost fourteen dollars), set on four legs and formally anointed as coffee tables. The proud owners will blithely disregard the three hundred dollars it cost for the carpenter in Pittsburgh to affix the legs, plus the tips to get it from the antique shop to the airport to home, and will happily show off their "fourteen-dollar table."

The success of a vacation geared to the needs of the shopper depends upon the feeling that you can safely indulge yourself without being greedy and that you cannot expect any achievement beyond the immediate gratification of the transaction itself. You must trust your own judgment about your real needs and depend upon your ability to give, to acquire and to pay the price. In addition, you must accept the fact that probably the only "bargain" will be in personal satisfaction—Peruvian blankets can often be bought for less in Chicago than in Cuzco.

Yet the veteran shopper must also face up to the reality that not everyone likes to shop. Some claim to grow dizzy, tired and irritable in a store. They cannot choose, they cannot act. Worse, many of them equate the act of shopping with throwing money away. Birthdays, Christmas presents, shopping for Mother's Day and a whole host of similar past catastrophes from long ago, may make a person balk like a mule at the entrance to a department store. When transported to a vacation, such an attitude becomes an obvious invitation to calamity.

Consequently, when you are traveling with such an individual, you can either go off on your own, or if you are willing and patient, you can attempt to introduce that person to the joys of your sport. For this latter option, a special set of rules must be followed. The secret shopping impulse that lies buried within everyone needs to be uncovered. Each has *something* that stirs his or her interest and stimulates curiosity. Even the most grudging have a secret—unrecognized passion for records, books, bath towels, chocolate or garden tools.

Whatever it might be, the discovery and reinforcement of this hidden urge obviously takes considerable perseverance. But the effort is worthwhile. Once uncovered, there can be a trade-off between forays to that special place (the garden shop or the bookstore) and explorations of the more traditional kinds of vacation shopping. Where there might otherwise have been discord, there can now be harmony.

At the opposite extreme, you may be traveling with a compulsive shopper, one who is hyperexcited and forever on the move. This type will not rest until all the garden tools in the area have been carefully picked over and considered in an intense search for the very best one at the very best price. The compulsive person needs to scour every store, looking at all sorts and condition of garden tools, turning them over, holding them up to the light, appraising them and arguing over them. The purchase only comes at the end of the day when the stores are about to close, and then it is only made with reluctance. Unfortunately, all this compulsion works no better than overeating or indulging in any other form of addictive behavior.

One possible solution, both for the individual unable to shop as well as for the one who cannot get enough, is to set firm limits in advance. Before the trip, make it clear that a certain amount of time shall be devoted to prowling through stores: no less than the agreed time for the first type, no more than the agreed time for the second. Although such restrictions sound counter to the whole idea of an undemanding holiday, establishing them may be the only way of avoiding the tensions and arguments that can destroy an entire holiday.

The excitement of shopping is the excitement of a treasure hunt. The traveler need only remember that shopping on a vacation, just like any other holiday activity, is really a form of play; a pleasant exercise whose only goal should be the enjoyment of the game.

The Homeland Vacation:
Back to Where It All Began

As Marcel Proust observed in *Remembrances of Things Past*, even something as inconsequential as eating pastry dipped in tea can resonate irresistibly through all the corridors of memory and feeling. This is the emotion rekindled for many by a visit to an ancestral homeland, a return to the place of their own birth or to the seat of family origins. There, at every step and with every smell, inner doors long shut and bolted swing open.

For most people, "going home" means returning to the country of their parents. Another familiar form of going home is the religious pilgrimage—to Jerusalem, Rome, Mecca or India. Such a journey is not to the source of a family heritage but to the home of spiritual identity. It is an opportunity to gain a sense of belonging while at the same time deepening feelings of self-knowledge.

In either of these cases, what most distinguishes the homeland vacation is the long perspective it brings. It is a time and a place for emotional involvement, for experiencing the resonances of a place and for embracing the memory and the history of the roots of the self.

Yet there are some people who wish to be unlike their family and their ancestors, and there are those who reject all notions of a spiritual or intellectual past. Their strongest desire is not to be limited by an inherited life-style or code of behavior.

They shy from contact with their origins as if such contact would rob them of a hard-won break with the past.

Leaving home is a necessary act of rebellion for everyone, an end to childhood and the beginning of an independent life. A premature return to that place can revive battles that were never won or result in an admission of defeat. Thus, a person needs to prepare, consciously or unconsciously, years before taking this step. He must explore and expand himself in the present before attempting contact with the past. He must have won the battle to be himself.

For this reason, a visit to the homeland is part of the emotional growth that vacationers will generally seek in mid-life. Some sense that they are nearing the time when they must become more generous to younger generations, that they must now share their secrets. Others feel that they must return once again to the memories of their past. Most will finally feel enough security in their own present to challenge the past.

But sometimes the traveler's investment in such a visit is high enough to insure disappointment. Many people build up such expectations of the return to the land, the folk, the tribal feelings, that they become distressed at the mundane reality they find. They are crushed not to be transported into their idealized visions; that hidden emotions do not swell up at the grave of each ancestor, at the site of every temple. They wonder just what they are suffering from that prevents them from feeling their roots.

Some idealization is necessary to cover the long emotional distance to the homeland. But it should not be allowed to spill over into the construction of rigid images too far in advance. Do not imagine that you will find Jesus still walking about in Nazareth, or that the village dances in Yugoslavia are not altered for tourist consumption, or that Great-Aunt Charity is as old and gracious as expected. A little irony might prove a helpful counterbalance to nostalgia and sentimental distortion.

If it is properly prepared for and carried out, the homeland vacation offers a unique opportunity for uncovering the paths of those who walked before us and who left trails for us to follow. You will see how much they endured in their struggle to build the farm in Michigan, in their seasick voyage across the Atlantic or in scraping savings for a new life out of their sweat in Naples. Going home, the traveler feels a deep communion with those fathers and mothers who came before, a richer appreciation of the present.

Weekends

Once the weekend was nothing more than an automatic break from the job, a chance to sleep late and read the paper in bed. But today many have transformed Saturday and Sunday into opportunities to do something instead of nothing. They have built into their lives the concept of the "leisure weekend," a time for hard learning and hard playing and, ideally, for personal growth.

These mini-vacations might include a stopover following a business trip to a distant city, a weekend at a second home or shared rental in the country. There are also the more unfamiliar "unwinder weekends," "cruises to nowhere" and "refresher weekends." Their purpose is to offer pleasurable engagement and activity in strong enough doses to counter the pressures of a hectic work week.

An unstructured weekend of just two days away from home and the circumstances of daily living can provide relaxation and expand interests and friendships, all at a relatively low cost. Yet there are some people who arrive at such weekends filled with dread. They are suffering from the "weekend neurosis," a complex of symptoms triggered by an inability to deal with unstructured time. With their school or work week so tightly organized, these individuals are simply unable to function without a structure that tells them how to behave.

The very anticipation of unplanned time will set these people off on a whole string of anxieties. They begin by feeling irritable, depressed and restless; they might end up suffering abdominal pains and headaches.

At least some variation of this neurosis lies within many individuals. Even while at home, it is not uncommon for the Sunday blues to set in. Saturday is busy with shopping, cleaning and odd jobs around the house. But Sunday is a free day and unsettled feelings are stirred as you try to shift gears into dealing with this open block of time. Many people effectively (but not very healthfully) avoid this by watching a string of football games or tennis matches on television, insulating themselves from their leisure time (and their families).

The remedy is a strong mix of self-encouragement (it's all right to relax; in fact, I owe it to myself and to others in order to be more productive later) coupled with some thoughtfully chosen activities—a walk, sketching, meeting friends, seeing a movie. Through activities such as these, it is possible to work out the inner tensions and move toward that state of relaxation which is essential to any true leisure.

The easy availability of these mini-vacations lulls some into feeling that a single, extended vacation is unnecessary, even redundant. The problem with such an attitude is that studies have revealed that for a vacation to be of most benefit, it must be extended for at least one week. The first two or three days are devoted to the unwinding process, the gradual letting go of the routines of daily living. Not until the third or fourth day is there a real separation and an unhindered participation in the new environment.

Once its nature and its limits are understood, the weekend can be a significant opportunity for leisure time. If individuals have been pressed into a production-oriented way of living, they must just as firmly press themselves out of it. They need to develop a healthy play ethic to complement the work ethic which dominates their lives. Here the weekend vacation can be especially important. Being an alternative to the full-scale vacation, it is a chance to ease out of the rat race gently, without the attendant pressures of preparing for a week or two away from home.

What these few days can provide is the essential mid-point between the week on the job and the week at the resort. Without treating the period as an all-out holiday, you can use the weekend to acclimate yourself to the idea of longer vacations. By not cramming all the activities of a ten-day span into just two or three, you will learn how to manage your leisure time. Understanding that several short trips cannot function as a single long trip, you will better appreciate the value of a full vacation. Finally, as you discover all these things, you will also find that you are making better use of the weekends themselves. You will have uncovered the narrow path out of the dread instilled by the weekend neurosis.

CHAPTER FOUR

❧ *Planning*

You have decided on the kind of vacation you would like—it may be a camping trip in Wales, Club Med in Greece, a tiny resort in New York State or two weeks in New Mexico. Whatever the decision, you have probably begun to experience the first delights of your vacation. All of the fantasies of meeting new people, of the exotic sights awaiting you and of the sheer pleasure in separation from the daily routine fills each day with reverie. These fantasies and daydreams are in a sense *trial actions*, allowing a person to confront an event mentally before encountering it in fact. Working through the varied steps, it is likely that some unexpected defects, traps and errors will become clear—and be corrected.

But another prevacation step is still necessary. After your head is attuned, the focus must turn to practical matters. This is when the tone for the entire vacation is set and the hidden kinks from the planning eliminated. Now begins the actual process of final selections and preparations. In many of its more tedious aspects, this preparation for a vacation may seem only routine. But the following pages reveal an essential part of the vacation experience. Adequate planning, although it cannot assure a successful holiday, is perhaps the best defense of all against a disappointing one.

The Travel Agent: Clerk or Guide?

There are two ways to make use of an agent. The first and easiest of these is to advise him or her of the general scope of the intended trip—whether skiing or swimming, for example —and then sit back and let all the details be worked out without any further participation. This option, while sparing the traveler the bother of decision making, confers blind faith on someone who may be (and probably is) largely ignorant of individual personality needs. Since travel agents are, after all, in the business of knowing about the location of vacation spots and about the logistics of reaching them, does it really make sense to rely so heavily on their opinions of personal needs?

In truth, the travel agent is in no way equipped or qualified to deal with the hidden structure of a client's personality. His real function is to help plot out a tour map—not to decide on the character of the trip.

Yet, and this is the second way to make use of an agent, if the traveler is careful to retain personal authority over the experience, such outside assistance can be used very effectively.

With such control the vacation is no longer in danger of being used either for profit or to satisfy the vicarious needs of the travel agent.

This control should include shopping around among several travel agents before settling on the one who is exactly right for you and for your needs. Then, after selecting one, the process may begin. First, it is a sound idea to have at least one preliminary discussion before booking the actual trip. Such consultation can iron out any lingering misunderstandings and insure that the two of you will not be working at cross purposes when the time comes for concrete arrangements. Once the various options, excursions, packages and the like have been thoroughly talked out, all the information should be taken home and reviewed—alone—before any irrevocable decisions are reached. Then another trip to the agent, but this time only to smooth and finalize the already agreed to itinerary. Such a deliberate method is probably the single way that the traveler can truly feel that the coming trip is a private matter: individually thought out, individually planned and (soon to be) individually implemented.

Eventually, as you and the agent become more familiar with each other, this laborious detail work can be replaced by a kind of shorthand. After booking you on several trips, the agent should be able to interpret your desires without requiring your elaborations. By that point, the two of you will have formed a team based on mutual understanding.

Getting in Shape

A frequent routine of the preparation period for some people is the time devoted to assembling the "right" wardrobe—and then losing enough weight to fit into it. While many look upon these functions with anxiety, shopping and dieting are both *significant* and *positive* elements in creating the aura that necessarily surrounds a successful vacation experience.

Many people are, or at least think they are, overweight, and the reducing impulse is almost a national obsession. But there is even a deeper motive behind a prevacation weight loss or a general physical toning up. If the holiday is a very special time, then all aspects of the person should be in top condition as well. Preparing the body for this singular period is similar in many ways to the practice of anointment for religious rituals in earlier civilizations. Vacationers acting in this way are almost purifying themselves for a hoped-for reunion with that more perfect part of their being that is allowed to emerge freely but once or twice a year.

If you do not feel all that terrific about your self-image, the vacation is the perfect time to set it right. The holiday memory will linger, reinforcing positive emotions and instilling pride in the recollection of accomplishment. Months afterward, when it is not so easy to feel glamorous while fighting rush-hour traffic, picking up and delivering the Little League team, shoveling snow from the driveway or cleaning the oven, you can glance back over the holiday photographs and see how it once was possible—and will be again—to match an inner ideal with the physical self. At such times, getting your body together for a vacation becomes well worth whatever effort it takes.

Clothing is an important contributor to the creation of a successful body image, but it is a tricky one to deal with. For one thing, it is probably impossible to come up with an objective measurement of what constitutes the "proper" dress in each situation. There are just as many people on the slopes wearing jeans and fishnet sweaters as there are others outfitted from head to toe in the latest clinging ski outfits. The only so-lution is to think it through beforehand; think about what you will need for the trip and what you will feel most com-fortable in at your destination. Then plan your wardrobe ac-cordingly. While clothes may or may not make the man or woman, they are the visible signs of inner desires and, on a va-cation particularly, no one wants to get those signs wrong. The time is much too short for a correction.

Taking this one step further, imagine the difficulties con-fronting the happy skier who decides to join his companions for a July weekend at the shore. When he arrives, he suddenly realizes that he is unable to sustain his confidence without a full costume to cover up. So he spends his days on the beach and in the sun in the grip of uneasiness; he is argumentative with his friends and generally hostile toward his surroundings. What this man has failed to recognize is that he feels uncom-fortable simply because he is feeling undressed and exposed. Never mind that a scanty costume is entirely appropriate for the surroundings; this is not appropriate for him.

The lesson of this story is that a lot of anxiety can be spared if only you remember whom you are doing it all for. The style you choose, the extra five pounds you lose, whatever external preparations you go through, must always be for yourself alone.

The Last Minute Blues: Terrors of the Week Before

Is this the right place? Is this the right time? Is this the best way to get there? Are these the right people to go with?

Change in any form produces anxiety and insecurity. Ev-

eryone feels a little uneasy during separations and in anticipation of any new venture. It's human. The problem comes
when these natural qualms are mistaken for real concerns ra-
tionally arrived at. Some people will avoid acting on even the
most well constructed of plans simply because of a few gnaw-
ing doubts, too vague to put into words.

The last few days before a vacation is a time when un-
verbalized emotions about separation from familiarity, and insecurity about decisions run close to the surface and may
erupt. It might begin a full week before, marked by unusual
concern about the coming holiday, the soon-to-be-deserted
home front, or unfinished work left behind on the job. Occa-
sionally, instead of being experienced directly, these pressures
may be converted into (or covered up by) bickering or outright fights with a traveling companion, spouse, or children. In
this case, the calm that took place before the storm might
never be reclaimed, while the real cause of that tempest might
never be discovered.

It is essential, in other words, to identify and to understand
these doubts as natural symptoms of the period of *separation
anxiety* that precedes most holidays. Often the solution lies in
thinking through the questions yourself or in talking about
them with as much detachment as can still be mustered with a
companion.

At this stage, a thorough review of other trips and of previous ways of coping with change can go a long way toward
isolating the more specific causes of anxiety. Some will discover that they are bothered by the mere thought of the coming separation from the familiar. The act of recognizing their
concern then will enable them to work on it.

Sometimes patient review will uncover planning flaws, the resolution of which can lead to a revitalization of the entire experience. There was, for example, a woman who constructed a complex itinerary for her coming trip through Italy, a country she knew well from previous visits. She had worked through the details exactly—the airplane connections, the hotel reservations and the tours. She thought that it all suited her personality and her particular needs to perfection, and yet "something" kept bothering her. She decided to explore her feelings.

The last trip, clearly the best, had been spent on a leisurely tour through the southern countryside capped off by three days on the Italian Riviera. But this time she was determined to catch up on all she had missed on prior visits. So she had scheduled a hectic round of museum visits, sight-seeing and hopping across the country by air.

With all this activity, as she thought about it, there was no time allotted to pure leisure, no time for relaxing on the beach or in a city with books to read and with no pressuring time table to follow. Yet these unstructured times were just what had made the previous visit so memorable. This new insight was the "something" that had been bothering her. With this understanding, her doubts lifted and, by modifying her itinerary slightly, she was able to give herself free time and again feel comfortable with her trip and pleased with her arrangements.

The few quiet hours given over to review of preparations proved the salvation of this woman's entire holiday. In exchange for what was really a very small effort, she was able to realize very great rewards.

Beyond Getting There:
Set the Rhythm

One important, but often overlooked, function of the preparatory period is *setting* the *overall rhythm* for the entire vacation. The value of proper physical and medical preparation is obvious, but what about the emotions? What's the use of arriving in Paradise alive and well yet not being really ready to enjoy it? Some subtle areas of emotional preparation have already been touched on and others will be in the course of subsequent chapters, but one additional thought here might be helpful.

Obviously, the week before most vacations is a hectic time. With shopping and with arranging things on the job and at home to accommodate your absence, there might not seem enough hours in the day to get everything done. A valuable suggestion for coping with this problem can be recalled from school days when many teachers suggested that all studying for an exam should be completed *prior* to the day before the test, thus allowing a period free to set the right tone and mood for the examination itself.

Similarly, it would be helpful to most people if they were to complete all the physical preparations some time before the holiday is to begin. Then the last few days can be loose and relatively anxiety free, allowing for the construction of a frame of mind upon which to build the trip itself.

Yet a caveat is in order here. Some people, in order to deal with and reduce prevacation anxieties, purposely leave things until the very last minute, building up an emotional head of steam to carry into the actual holiday thereby damaging all possibility of genuine relaxation. Should you be one of these, the task is clear. *Recognize the uneasiness* and save a few little tasks for those last several days. But seek to control the anxiety through *orderly activity* rather than by frenzied racing around. In this way, you can avoid the self-defeating condition of beginning a vacation at such a fever pitch that it will take you half the vacation (at least) to relieve the tension and start having a good time.

The Details (One): Taking Pictures

For most travelers, a camera—be it Instamatic or Nikon—is a way of extending memories beyond the journey itself. Some also see the little black box, that badge of the traveler hanging around the neck or clutched in the hand, as lending credibility to the role of the vacationer, telling everyone in sight that, "I'm not working, I'm not getting paid for this, so my relaxed pace and my leisurely demeanor are not signs of laziness; I am just a hard-working citizen set free on vacation." Others display their cameras (and camera bags, interchangeable lenses, and rolls of film) for reasons that are quite nearly the opposite. These people are declaring themselves photographers as well as tourists, recording valuable pictures, not just taking holiday snapshots.

But the camera is more than a kind of outward badge. For some travelers, it is a means of setting themselves apart from the experience before them. Instead of participating in the pleasures of the moment, these people observe it all through the tiny hole in their black box. They manage to reduce the experience and keep it at a safe distance, limiting their enjoyment to that of an observer or of a dispassionate reviewer. This may prove a helpful protection, since some travelers are

very anxious about any kind of new experience and retic
about the possibility of involvement. Being behind the can
lens, therefore, offers that degree of protection necessary
make heightened sensations more acceptable. Such a pe
feels safe there, behind the camera mask, because back t
no one else can see the emotion.

But awareness of this need to hide or to provide dist
should allow for some control of "shutter mania" and g
against a post-vacation feeling of having been so busy ta
pictures that some of the actual pleasures of contact
missed. If you are prone to this distancing tactic, then d
the preparation period you might want to set some adv
limits on yourself. Try reducing the amount of film
taken along and resolve to make a conscious effort to re
from returning home with the entire trip reduced to p
with very little of it inside yourself.

The Details (Two):
Carrying the Medicine Cabinet

Many busy people neglect having physical/medical
lems resolved until the last minute, until the pain or t
comfort is too much to bear. They can't find the tim
think it will go away by itself, or else they are students
"suffer in silence" school. Whatever the exact cause
malady, such people feel that they can easily deal wi
home where modern medicine awaits their every call.

Once on vacation, however, things may be different
different. Depending where the patient is, help may b
ble only in the form of a medical missionary who visit
week—and was just here yesterday—or some shady c
whose specialty seems to be recommending treatmen

heard of by the American Medical Association. Or there may simply be no doctor at all. And even if the care is as good as anything available back home (or better), no one enjoys having a complete stranger poking around his body, telling him things he may not want to hear in a language he may not understand.

So the foremost medical rule on vacation must be: get new eyeglasses if you need them (and think about carrying an extra pair), have the tooth filled, refill the needed prescription —all *before you go*. Maybe the common cold cannot be prevented, maybe the minor irritants of daily living cannot be totally avoided, but those incipient, imminent medical problems certainly can be avoided on a holiday.

But what about the everyday virus, what about all those little aches and pains? For dealing with them, every tourist should have along a personally developed first aid kit. Included should be Band-Aids and aspirin, of course, as well as various medications suited to one's own health, past experience and to the specific conditions likely to be encountered at the vacation spot. Finally, a list of local doctors should be obtained, in case of the *not*-so-common cold. Getting sick is not a necessary precondition for vacationing in a far-off place; but then, neither is it an impossible circumstance. It is better to be ready than sorry.

Travel Togetherness: Planning with the Others

Everyone has a different approach and different expectations in planning and preparing for a vacation. Consequently, if going with the family or with friends, it is best to *iron it all out in advance*.

How? The most direct way is to discuss the role each member would like to assume during the preparation and, later, on the journey itself. This will not be as easy as it sounds, for some people have secret selves, just waiting for any chance to emerge. What a person does in real life, therefore, may have no bearing on hidden desires. An individual surrounded all day every day with designs for superhighways, locations for shopping centers and ideas for relocating neighborhoods may want to do nothing on holiday but lie back and let it all happen, without a trace of a plan, without a hint of organization. At the same time, the most scatterbrained and disorganized member of the group might suddenly get organized, thrilled at the chance of being responsible, as "tour director," for the trip.

Once some sort of general plan has emerged—and it should not get too structured: this is a holiday and not a military operation—the time has come for everyone to sit down together and discuss individual goals for the vacation. One value in such meetings is the fun of talking about holiday expectations and hearing the others talk about their desires, but there are other advantages as well.

Each person should go over his or her thoughts about the experience to come; about how much time they want alone, together, shopping, swimming, sunning or reading; about their expectations and their wishes. While some enjoy doing things with people on vacations and love the noise and the bustle, others will long for occasional periods of privacy within all that communion. So it is essential, before starting out, to know who wants what and when they want it. At these advance sessions, it is also good to go over prior vacations similar to the current one (everyone has stories to tell about past holiday experiences, both good and bad) in order to learn about any particular difficulties, individual aversions, personal ways of doing things and any last suggestions about getting the most from this coming trip.

Whenever children are included, it is also necessary to consult with them during the preparation period. Consultation will give them some sense of responsibility for the success of future events and give them time to prepare for the newness of the coming experience—which will no longer be so "new" now that everybody has talked it over.

The point here is that preparation must be for everyone. Otherwise, if any members of the travel party are left out of this period, the entire vacation may be put askew, with someone's needs either forgotten or slighted. Neither need happen.

Think Before You Say Yes: Alone or Together?

For everyone, there are times when the strongest urge is to get away somewhere by yourself, to go off without company and without schedules.

Still, many people are nagged by persistent doubts whenever a secret longing for solitude comes over them. They feel guilty about the preference to reject the generous invitation to share a week at the shore or in the mountains. These solo vacationers had been programmed to view their holiday as a time of almost predestined togetherness. It makes them feel guilty about this new itch or perhaps that real need to do something alone. Two examples will help to illustrate the situation.

Suppose that your companion is going off to Florida for a week and wants you to come, but you would rather go skiing.

If you agree to go to Florida in spite of your real desires, will you be bitter the whole time, dreaming of short lift lines and deep powder? Or will you manage to come to terms with the sun and the surf and enjoy the company?

Or else imagine that someone from work asks you and your spouse to spend your vacation at their summer house on the beach. It means a very cheap holiday, but you had hoped that both of you would be able to get away alone this year. Besides you don't feel much like being in a situation where office problems will be a daily topic of conversation and the politics of the job will hang over you for two weeks. Having already spent one weekend with this couple, you suspect that all this is inevitable. Should you go despite your misgivings, and hope for the best?

In both of these cases, the direction of your thoughts has been toward rejection of the invitations, but a sense of politeness and social obligation is pushing you the opposite way. Instead of your guilt, what you must remember is that it is never selfish to need occasional space for yourself, space to be alone in and space to listen to your private self. Without such moments of retreat, you may become hostile and anxious all the rest of the year. By submitting to an imagined social obligation for two weeks, you will be giving up on a very real personal obligation for the other fifty; *an obligation to renew yourself* and, thus, become a better social companion.

Solitude is not, in any sense, a luxury; it is a periodic necessity. Learn to recognize the need when it strikes and, further, learn how to act upon it. Saying no to a holiday offered by others is much easier once you understand that this special time is yours alone, a time to be used only for meeting your own desires. Anything else is secondary.

A Matter of Timing: When Not to Go

If there is a right place and a right duration for a holiday, is there also a right time? Is there ever a period in anyone's life when it is a mistake to take time off? Briefly: Yes, there is.

Most people go on vacation when they want to sample some new experience or when they want to relax at some special place. They may be run down by daily routine, but they are not defeated by it. The holiday is not their last hope for recovery but is instead their best hope for renewal. Their idea of a vacation is of a *quest after pleasure*.

For others, it is more likely to be an *escape from unresolved pressures*. They take time off only when they have "had enough" of their daily routine, when tensions have passed the limits of tolerance or when they are still in the depths of suffering over a recent loss. They may be obeying the modern folk remedy to "put it all behind you; go off for a couple of weeks; try to forget about it." But, unfortunately, by the time of that advice, it is usually too late.

A vacation is a new, revitalizing and relaxing experience, *intended* to be different from the rest of the year. It is *not* meant for dealing with stress or for coping with personal problems. When asked to fulfill such a need, it will almost inevitably end up infected by the very symptoms it was supposed to cure. When people have passed through the *critical level of stress*, no amount of vacationing is able to dissipate the anxieties adequately. The *critical level of stress* is the point at which tension is so high it will only contaminate the holiday itself. Getting away then will, in the long run, just make it worse.

The important thing is to recognize the danger period. The increasing sense of irritability, the difficulty "getting it together" each morning, the feeling of not wanting to return to work after lunch or of not wanting to face the day at all, these may be ascribed to exhaustion or boredom and may, in fact, be taken as signals that it is time to take a holiday. In truth, however, it is already too late.

When the *critical level* is nearing or has already been passed, a special regimen must be followed; a regimen that does *not* include an extended vacation. Instead, the proper method of dealing with any kind of pressure involves slowly working through the stressful incident or memory until it is fully out in the open and gone from the system. This requires two processes: stepping down tension through the use of one or two weekends away and confronting the stressful event. The most appropriate setting for confrontation is not a faraway, sunlit beach but in familiar surroundings where the troubling emotions may be dealt with directly. Sharing with a trusted friend helps.

Then, as the process of resolution occurs, there is a gradual and appreciable reduction of the pressures until they are no longer a dominant part of life, and a happier future once more seems possible. Refusing to face the problem and going off on a vacation merely insures its continuation and the destruction of an experience which should be devoted, presumably, to pleasure.

If they are timed right, vacations can serve a valuable function *after* one of these difficult periods. Gauging the moment correctly is all important here: At the height of the suffering, when escape seems most needed, it will serve the purpose least. Only when the emotions are much reduced and the sufferer is on the way up again is it time to get away. For then the vacation experience can lead to real renewal; it will be experienced as an act of the present unburdened by the memories of the past.

In all of this discussion, there has been one common thread. If it is to succeed, a vacation must be seen as a complement *to* life; it is not a replacement *for* life or an escape *from* life. To expect anything else is to invite disappointment.

Aftermath

Very few people enjoy coming home from a vacation, but it is something worth thinking about and planning for. Coming home means separation from a good time, the loss of new acquaintances and a hard psychological shift from play back to work. The holiday has been a pleasurable break from routine, and its ending means a return to the pressures of daily living.

Many try to ease themselves through the homecoming by extending the process, by planning special leisure activities for the time following their return. They give themselves something to look forward to—a dinner out with friends, a visit to the theater, a day trip the next weekend. And so they reward themselves for any improvement in their dealing with job or school problems. Through the promise of future leisure opportunities, they are reinforcing the calmer values brought back from the holiday.

Sharing vacation pictures, or stories also extends vacation pleasure. Nearly everyone enjoys living through other people's stories of adventure in distant lands. The admiration of friends and relatives as they pore over the photographs and listen to those exotic stories brings back a part of the wonder and the joys experienced on the vacation itself.

These strategies build a period of transition into the end of the holiday and are among the best ways of smoothing the return home. A good transition from being away to being home can, in fact, be as important to the well being of the traveler as most stages of the holiday itself. This is the point when the meanings are set and where the memories are solidified; this is the point that clarifies what the vacationer will bring away from the experience.

Often, this transition period can be best incorporated into the structure of the vacation itself. If the holiday has been to a distant place and there must be a lengthy drive home, for instance, it might be wise to break up the trip by spending a night on the road. Such a stopover, being not quite holiday and not quite homelife, is a time to decompress between stations, to collect the memories of what has been and to prepare for what will be.

Another variety of transition is the establishment of a "buffer zone" between the end of the holiday and the beginning of work or school. Give yourself some free time at home before the turmoil begins anew—time to catch up on local gossip, sift through the accumulated mail, to call friends and relatives with the first wave of vacation stories. This buffer will be a cushion for the shift back into your routine.

The necessary objective here is to bring some perspective to the experience, to bring context to the trip and to make getting home a much less painful and more natural episode. The point is to make playtime flow into worktime with as little sputtering and grinding of gears as possible.

By lessening the trauma of coming home, you will find yourself able to review and understand the quality of the vacation adventure and position it securely within your own mind. The mistakes of last time need not be the mistakes of next time.

CHAPTER FIVE

🌺 The Spoilers: Turning Good into Bad

Spoiling is basically the process—using a variety of means—of turning something good into something bad; precisely the opposite of what vacations are supposed to be all about. Asked if he or she anticipates a potentially pleasant experience, the spoiler is likely to give a qualified answer. Either, "Yes, I would like to take a vacation, but what about the children?" or else, "Sure, I want to get out of the snow and into the sun, but what if I don't meet anyone and can't enjoy myself?" Spoiling is generally induced by fear: fear of the unknown, of travel, of disease, of loss, even fear of death.

The techniques people use to avoid their fears may include

a simple refusal to make any advance plans or dumping all the preparation on travel companions. Their hidden fears may emerge as accusations at the first suspected mishap: "Just look what you made us do." Or it may take the form of constant reminders of imagined dangers. There are worries about hijackers on the airplane, about the dollar not going as far in Germany any more, or about how rotten last year's vacation was. The more reasonable these risks sound the better, for then they will be more difficult to refute. But the logic of such vacation qualifiers is not the issue. The spoiler is using them, not because of their logic or probability, but to undermine all secure feelings about a coming holiday. Such talk tends to get a travel companion so unnerved that he or she may explode in heated anger and cancel the trip altogether. Which, of course, is just the point.

While spoilers disguise their true purpose by appearing in a number of different masks, it is possible to isolate the major areas of their activity and learn how to remedy them. The most common of these spoiling traits stems from *separation anxiety*, an uneasiness about a loss of the familiar. It is a complex affliction, one with a number of different symptoms, and one that is worth considerable attention.

Separation Anxiety

Everyone is aware of the sadness and emptiness caused by a move to a new place, by going off to college, by changing jobs or by ending a marriage. But few are aware that similar feelings emerge when one takes time off for an extended vacation. Even anticipated pleasure is not enough to overcome still unmastered fears lingering from early childhood: fears of separation from the home, from the family, from familiar patterns.

Anxiety in some form is only normal and is experienced by nearly everyone. Yet while most people in the general course of maturation develop healthy strategies to overcome these stresses, many others never seem to be able to leave home or children comfortably. Such unresolved separation anxiety is one of the major reasons for avoiding extended vacations, for aborting a vacation in midstream, for never taking any kind of holiday, or, in the case of couples, for never leaving the children at home. There are several different disguises of this "goal" of never having to risk a vacation, phobias being one of the most common.

PHOBIAS

The first difficulty with phobias is learning to recognize them as such and to realize that fear can be an automatic response to certain places and activities, or even to *thinking* about such places and activities. If flying, visiting New York City, or climbing a mountain makes the pulse pound with dread and makes the blood run cold in anticipation of the calamities ahead, then this is a phobic reaction.

The poorest response for anyone so afflicted is to deny that fear is involved and cling to the pretense that flying—because of lost baggage, New York, because of dirty streets—and mountains—because of thin air—are all objective evils and that no sensible person would have anything to do with any of them. Such defensive attitudes only cloud the real issue and insure that the phobia will have its widest possible impact.

Consider the wife of a wealthy zipper manufacturer who reluctantly agreed to a trip to Israel with her husband and their two children. She is phobic about flying—although she denies it—and has made herself into an expert on jet plane disasters, dividing them by aircraft type, location, airline and number of corpses. She will do nothing about her fear of flying—which she, after all, considers a reasonable conclusion reasonably arrived at—and so the family separates for long trips.

In this case, she sails to Haifa with the children while her husband flies off by himself. When they finally meet in Israel, he is furious at her for the three-week separation and his anger overshadows both the vacation and their relationship. For her part, she uses his animosity, which she professes not to understand, as an excuse to avoid him again. The vacation has been ruined before it begins.

The fear underlying this woman's particular phobia, and which she refuses to recognize, is her anxiety about *any* experience that might somehow lead to a loss of control. The avoidance is an attempt at reaching for protection; it is her guard against engagement in any form. It not only spoils this trip to Israel, but it also spoils all chances for sudden excitement. Which is exactly the way she wants it.

Evasions such as this one can fool both the self and others some of the time, but they do nothing about helping the individual through the submerged fears. With phobias, one technique which has been found effective is that of behavior modification, the conscious altering of an established pattern. For example (and to maintain fear of flying as an illustration), the phobic individual might sit down with a friend and make a list of all things about airplanes that come to mind, ranking them according to the degree of fear they each inspire. These can range from the mildest (building a model airplane or seeing a picture of an airplane) to the most anxiety provoking (looking down at the empty ocean from thirty thousand feet). Once the list has been completed, each of the items should be thoroughly discussed and its potential for provoking fear carefully analyzed.

The process may take months, for one should proceed step by step from the model to visiting an airport and perhaps sitting in a real airplane. Behavior modification has proven so successful in dealing with this particular phobia, that a number of organizations have incorporated these techniques at meetings around the country. The goal is not to "conquer" fear but to be able to live with it and to cope with it; the key to coping lies in understanding.

Another approach, both for this and for other phobias, is to try psychotherapy. While therapy is expensive, it is far less costly than denial, ruined vacations and years of nameless dread. Experience should be held priceless. A world of fears bars the way to pleasure, and giving in to a phobia without a fight, without even an attempt at resolution, is an unnecessary mistake. Phobias, as we have suggested here, can be dealt with.

HYPOCHONDRIA

Another form of separation anxiety is hypochondria. This is the unreasoned fear of illness and can be just as effective as phobias in restricting vacation enjoyment. Here as well, self-knowledge is the indispensable way out, and denial is disastrous. If a person accepts that sore throats, constipation, head colds and the like are just as possible while traveling as they are anyplace else, realistic preparation can reduce both the symptoms (if they occur) and the fears. Just having the proper medication along (such as aspirin, decongestants, vitamins, a laxative) can bring needed security. The crucial decision with hypochondria is whether to be governed by secret fears or to take active control of the situation. The best approach is to gradually desensitize one's self by moving toward the center of the anxiety, one small step at a time.

Suppose a man is about to go off to Spain with his wife when he develops the sudden but sure feeling that the unfamiliar Spanish spices will be constipating, that prune juice will be unavailable and that, one thing leading to another, he will find himself with rectal cancer and without a doctor. To this man, it is as certain as Spanish sunlight: going to Spain equals rectal cancer.

His anguish is very real; there is a vivid picture in his mind of his wife shopping for little knickknacks while he spends the entire vacation stuck in their hotel room, waiting as death creeps ever closer. His gruesome imaginings magnify as the day of their departure draws near.

Yet, there are options to all his suffering. In this case, his wife can adopt a rational but tough method of fear reduction, taking her husband to a pharmacy to purchase prune preparations and similar medications, insuring him instant relief and comfort from even the most virulent spices. She can also get a list of the doctors and hospitals in Spain, including the names of the leading proctologists. By accepting his fears as fears and not dismissing them out of hand, she can reduce them and prevent her husband from abandoning the vacation altogether. For his part, he must be willing to accept this treatment and make every effort to understand his fears. A solution will not come easily; it must be attempted with persistence.

MISPLACED CONCERN

Even without specific phobias or hypochondria, some people manage to build separation anxiety into the vacation expe-

rience. They concentrate on things like the gas not being
turned off, or things left behind in the haste of departure,
things that might go wrong with the flight, at the airport, or
at the resort.

One way of countering this attitude, and one that many
travelers have found effective, is the development of an inner
dialogue. Fears can be faced and pressures exposed and a rational perspective developed. Thus, dangers can be confronted
or diminished. A typical "conversation" should go something
like this:

> *Listen, traveler, whose vacation is this?*
> "My vacation."
> *O.K. Do you want a good one or a bad one?*
> "I want a good one, of course."
> *Of course, you say. Well then, is scaring yourself by
> imagining disasters helping you to a good start?*
> "No, it's making things worse."
> *What would make things better?*
> "Thinking about something else; not clinging to awful
> images of what might happen. Just letting go."
> *What's stopping you then?*
> "My own anxiety."
> *Well, whose experience is this anyway?*
> "My experience."
> *And what are you doing to it?*
> "Spoiling it."
> *Can you stop spoiling it?*
> "Yes."
> *How?*
> "By focusing on the good."
> *Try it.*

"Well, the fire engines can put out the fire. The neigh-
bors will see the burglars and call the police. . . ."

*Wait a minute. Are these "solutions" any more real
than your fears?*

"Not much."

So try again.

"I'm imagining bad things because I'm scared. What's
real is that I'm safe and my plans are well made. I feel
healthy, and I'm off to a good place. The people will be
friendly and, even if there are mishaps, I've always handled
them well in the past and, besides, the other people I meet
will help out. It won't be as bad as all that. In fact, it
should be pretty good. I'm really looking forward to it."

Variations of this form can be useful in countering most
types of separation anxiety. When an individual can admit to
fears, he or she is really in contact with inner emotions.
Only then can there be any confidence that the secret dreads
will be resolved.

Separation anxiety will often show itself as *bickering*
between companions. Because such displays rarely appear before the trip has gotten under way, they cannot be resolved by
any prevacation soul searching. Yet they are as much in need
of resolution as any other form of anxiety,

If a woman visits her mother every year and her husband,
who hates going, will neither stay home alone nor let her go
by herself nor accept the idea of separate vacations, then the
stage is well set for bickering. He will begin to pick on his
mother-in-law while his wife defends her intently. They will
quarrel this way through the whole holiday, the way they always do.

This kind of separation anxiety results not from fear of the coming vacation but from the fear of risking change in their vacation routine. This couple is not only expressing hostility they might feel toward one another, but they are also secretly accusing their partner of their own fear of changing outworn habits.

If either of these spoilers could just say, "I am afraid," instead of, "You are bad," it would bring their dissatisfactions to the surface where they might be acted upon. But, as with all cases of separation anxiety, their denial will not allow them even this simple admission. And so they move on to the rage/glue game.

The Rage/Glue Game

Although it may take many forms, the essential meaning of the rage/glue conflict is that childish fears are in control. It may begin as separation anxiety, but this problem will magnify and expand its impact as time passes.

Resentment of change, fear of the new or the unknown, any unexpected encounter, may swamp an otherwise reasonable person. If not answered by reason, these tensions might lead to indiscriminate rage.

No sooner had Mr. and Mrs. G boarded their 707 for Stockholm than Mr. G began snarling at the stewardess, raging at the food and fuming over the line for the restroom. This was a trip that Mr. G was not sure he should be taking, he was uncertain of the climate in Scandinavia, and he didn't like flying over the ocean. Clearly, he was suffering from separation anxiety. But he did not know that. Nor did his wife when she impatiently told him to calm down, that things were not so bad and that he was making a spectacle of himself. This lack of sympathy only drove him to new heights of rage and he lashed out at Mrs. G, loudly calling her ignorant and stupid.

His words enraged her and she answered in kind by announcing to seats DEF that Mr. G is a boor, a failure and a terrible father to poor Priscilla. Both Mr. and Mrs. G are now thoroughly encapsuled in a mutual battle which carries them all the way across the Atlantic, through Sweden and all the way back home again.

What could they have done to defuse this unhappy situation before the explosion and lingering aftershocks? First of all, they needed to know more about themselves and more about each other.

For his part, Mr. G needed to know that he was afraid, that fear, not his wife, was the real enemy. He had to understand that his secret fears were turning into rage, and if he could express his anxiety, it would diminish.

Mrs. G had to discover that her husband was just scared and that he required an empathic response from her. She needed to know that his accusations were more from his fear than from any real complaint, and that she could helpfully give reassurance.

The destructive fact about the rage/glue game is that it is no longer capable of recognizing either wants or needs. It makes a person in its grip forget he is spoiling his own vacation.

The Subconscious Saboteur

Some people will invariably ruin a vacation before it has gotten under way or will abort it in midstream without really

trying to improve things. Everything seems to have been arranged perfectly for these people, and yet time after time
something goes wrong. Whatever it may be, they will make
no effort to correct it, but will scatter the blame about like
ragweed pollen, considering every mistake, no matter how
small and no matter how innocent, as a personal affront. They
will cut the holiday short and rush home, minds swirling with
complaints.

An older man, unmarried and the owner of a small retail
concern, described problems with his business which never allowed him, so he thought, to enjoy his vacations. While he
was a good and flexible planner, he usually returned from his
various trips feeling that his work had encroached on his vacation. Digging further into the problem, he described his back-
up arrangements for covering the business while he was away.
It soon became clear that lying within each plan, neatly and
subtly tucked away, was a potential booby trap. For instance,
if he hired someone to work for him just before going away,
he never investigated that individual's past record of absen-
teeism or honesty. Or, even if he had hired a reliable stand-in,
he forgot to leave adequate information about reordering or
about whom to contact in the event of some mechanical failure. Further, while he never failed to advise everyone of his
exact whereabouts, he also told them *never* to hesitate calling
if a problem, *any problem*, arose, and as a coup de grace to his
pleasure, he never failed to call the business daily, "just to be
sure everything was all right."

The sabotage mechanism here is right out in the open,
though the underlying cause may be less evident. Sometimes it
may be guilt that robs people of the possibility of enjoyment,
sometimes it is anxiety, sometimes it is fear. Whichever, all

share a common end: the avoidance of pleasure and the need to spoil it. Fortunately, it is an end that can be avoided.

This businessman, for instance, should examine his failed holidays objectively and then make some practical allowances. He should resolve to eliminate the booby traps he uncovers one at a time. He must make conscious decisions to hire (and then to train) a reliable vacation replacement, *not* to leave a number where he can be reached and, above all, *not* to call in every day. Only after these preparations have been completed and rigidly adhered to is there any hope to modify his emotions successfully.

Guilt

Guilt is probably the strongest spoiler of vacations. It can undermine all expectations of delight, whether great or small. It can be induced from anywhere, by anyone. It can be specific or random; justified or not.

Consider the feelings of the man who told his mother that he was finally going to realize the dream of his lifetime and visit Japan. "And leave me here to die all alone?" she asked harshly. When he told his business partner, that man retorted with a lengthy tirade against Japanese imports that were "ruining the whole industry." Rattled now, he turned to his minister for some solace. Instead he was treated to an angry denunciation of the Japanese who were sending "heathen cultists to convert Christian youth to idolators." How could he go *there*, the minister demanded to know.

How, this man asked himself after hearing these remarks, how could he ever have thought of flying off to Japan and damaging so many people?

This is the nature of guilt feelings. If this man is unable to keep his own perspective, then he may be crushed by them, the good will quickly turn to bad and Japan, the lifelong dream, will be put forever out of reach. The difficulty is that this kind of guilt does not result from a judicial decree. It may be the product of another's envy or fear, or it may be caused by some imagined failing with little basis in fact. The only resolution is to maintain an awareness of personal requirements. A vacation's purpose is to answer individual needs, and the only voice that has to be listened to is the voice of the self. To counter the words of guilt, a person needs to feel, "I deserve this good experience. I do enough for others. I am not hurting anyone."

If a person finds himself beginning a prevacation guilt trip that threatens to cancel or spoil his whole plan, there is one good rule to follow. Go and talk the situation over with a person who has recently been able to enjoy a similar kind of vacation. Since guilt is in the nature of an accusation that one "does not deserve" something good, it is fatal to try to get permission for going on a vacation from one's poor, old, lonely mother-in-law, jealous brother, or hard-pressed business partner.

A person who has recently enjoyed a vacation will not only be eager to share his own good experience, and thus reinforce the whole idea of trying to get a good vacation, but that friend will also be confirming that it is *not selfish to take care of oneself*. Such a friend can reinforce that inner faltering voice that begins to doubt whether this vacation idea is really okay. Guilt makes it difficult for a person to be his own best friend. To understand that is to be in the position of making a good move, instead of moving against oneself.

When that little guilty voice of the inner enemy says, "You don't deserve this vacation. You only worked fifty-three weeks this year," that is not the time to go visit another accuser, someone who is going to say, "I worked fifty-five weeks this year without a vacation." This is the time to visit Uncle Harry, who goes fishing for a month every year, and feels just fine about it.

Above all, a person prone to going on guilt trips instead of vacations should beware of making this hidden deal with the self: "Okay, you can go on the vacation, but make sure you do not enjoy it. Remember to focus on what is bad, and that way no one will envy you or accuse you of being selfish. Maybe you can lose your wallet or get sick." To focus on the bad is to pack too much guilt in the suitcase.

Idealization

Anyone who holds to a rigid and unwavering image of perfection, on vacation or anywhere else, is failing to remember that the grittiness of existence does not—and never can—quite resemble an ideal. Mud, delay, sunburn, lost property and indigestion are all part of the holiday experience; to the individual expecting only to be served perfection, the actual bill of fare will seem indigestible.

A certain amount of illusion is essential. In a way, the process is similar to adolescence: Unless the growing child idealizes the world, he or she will never leave home. Unless the adult partially idealizes the tasks ahead, they will never be attempted, and unless the vacationer hopes for a holiday renewal ahead, the trip will never be made.

In its most widely recognized form, idealization is the creation of an unapproachable goal, a standard of perfection against which all things are measured—and are doomed to fall short. For example, an older man, traveling with a group through Peru, was thoroughly chained to comparisons. While eating the good, crisp bread of Cuzco, he bellowed that a decent hamburger was not to be had in the whole worthless country. Then he lapsed into stories about apple pie, Texas, and Chicago, using them against the onslaught of alien food and images. The climax came at Machu Picchu.

To get there, one must take the train from Cuzco, winding through the gorge of the muddy, boiling Urubamba River amid the high meadows of sunny green cut through by the shadows of the Andes. The landscape modulates from rolling uplands to forest to jungle where red orchids spring out of the trees, confronting the passengers with sudden bursts of color. The whole area resonates with mystery, with the intermixed histories of Spaniard, Indian, and lordly Inca. The promise of ominous adventure hangs in the air as the train struggles higher and higher. Then, suddenly, there it is: the golden Inca city, hanging from the cliffs.

From the train depot there is still a dizzying, switchback ride up the side of a mountain to reach the strange walled place, a place whose function is still unknown. The traveler can feel nothing but reverence for these ancient people, for their having mastered this other-worldly landscape with their terraces and with their roads while suspended there, above the clouds like their sacred condors.

But this man would have nothing of it. As his companions clustered around, eagerly sharing the first awestruck glimpse, they heard him mutter wearily to himself, "This is nothing. The Grand Canyon is better." This man's secret longing to repeat an idealized past experience, spoils his participation in the present.

Choosing a destination is not quite the same thing as deciding one is really going to be there wholeheartedly, trying to get the most out of every opportunity to taste, touch and feel the new experience—whether it is exotic or a return to a familiar place in a different phase of one's life. On vacation, an attitude such as this man's means eternal disappointment. It means the traveler has forgotten that the holiday is for *him or her*, and that there are many roads to gratification to choose from, if only one will be open to them.

A subtler—though equally self-defeating—type of idealization is deciding that the perfect image is indeed unreachable and therefore should not even be risked. Some manage to put the means to satisfy vacations securely out of reach by choosing a genuinely impossible experience as IT—the secretly longed for event. Others will unconsciously hold back on their commitment to an attainable goal: perhaps by not saving for a vacation in Spain, or by not getting the information necessary for planning a trip to some special place.

All of these variations insure that, wherever one is and whomever one is with, the shining ideal simply cannot be met, or even approached. Such perfectionist attitudes clearly go against the purpose of any vacation; closing off any good option in the mind will inevitably close it off in fact.

Not Taking Responsibility

People are continuously tempted to try to find an easy substitute for self-knowledge and decision making. Two of these temptations are overreliance on the vacation industry and being seduced by the vacation industry.

OVERRELIANCE

Naturally, the vacation industry wants you to go where *it* is prepared to go. So they might decide that one year the Yucatan will be *the* new resort area. Soon the forces to transport available travelers there will be geared up: soon massive propaganda batteries will be unleashed—travel ads, magazine stories, films and stores displays. Soon going to the Yucatan will seem as inevitable as the weather. Everyone will be going, and everyone will love it. The trip will not be expensive; the new resort will provide all the conveniences of home; and package deals will make the whole idea too good to resist. A trip to the Yucatan will become a necessity for any "in" traveler.

But is this where you want to go? The vacation industry decides only when vacationers are uncertain of what they want or are unwilling to take the trouble of getting what they want. Take Mr. and Mrs. K.

Mr. and Mrs. K wanted to go to Peru but found that Rio comes with Peru, much like bacon comes with eggs. The only way they could avoid Rio and still get to Peru was by spending a week in Bolivia, which cost more and took longer. So it seemed easier to be "packaged" for a week in Rio. The result was that they both loved Peru, as they knew they would, and they both hated Rio, as they suspected they might. And they were angry with themselves for not spending more time in Peru.

The following summer, this couple resolved to do better and began by choosing a different travel agent, whom they approached with determination to be firmer and not to let their real desires slip away. Inevitably, they began seeing the same things happening all over again, like the revival of a once popular play, though now with a slightly different cast. More money-saving packages.

This time they were interested in spending the month of July at a quiet place near the ocean with easy access to tennis. They had been thinking of someplace like Martha's Vineyard. The agent began to smile: "The Vineyard? In July? Quiet?" She chuckled and Mr. K grew nervous. Well, maybe Portugal then; Portugal is good. The agent frowned, "It would cost over a thousand in airfare and besides, politically, Lisbon is a mess." So where is good then? The agent beamed: "HA-WAII." Hawaii was good. Cheap and good. They began to feel desperate; the Massachusetts coast was turning into Wai-kiki just the way the Peruvian Andes had turned into the beaches of Brazil. But what could be said against the unassailable logic of the twenty-one-day package tour? They ordered the tickets to Honolulu and tried thinking positive thoughts about pineapple. Mr. and Mrs. K had let themselves down again, not making a decision for themselves, taking the easier way. In Hawaii they got angry at each other.

It is easy to imagine being in their place. At times, every city and village seems to be turning itself into another tourist attraction, and all cultures, folkways, even industries are on display for the eager eye of the vacationer. The holiday universe is a vast and movable collection of images, of alternatives and of money-saving plans, making informed selection next to impossible unless the prospective client enters the agency with self-understanding. It takes courage for a person or a couple to defy the smooth logic of airline schedules and hotel packages, and to *plan* a trip, a *personal* trip. The important thing is to use the various aids of the vacation industry to suit your own purposes, but not at the expense of your desires. The travel agent, the package tours, the airlines, all have something to offer, but let the ideas expressed in Chapters 2 and 3 of this book be the basis for your decision—not what is available in July or on sale in December. Let the travel industry remain preoccupied with filling hotel rooms and airline seats. Your job is to fulfill yourself.

SEDUCTION

Being seduced by a brochure is another form of poor self-understanding. When Mr. and Mrs. Y decided to travel to a resort in Africa for their vacation, it was because of a marvelous brochure. But when, after a long and difficult flight, they arrived in the Ivory Coast, they found themselves confused.

They tottered from the plane, across the steaming tropical soil and onto the white Club Paradise bus that was to take them to their destination. At first, they were driven from the soaring arcs of aluminum, glass and concrete of the airport past a teeming slum of mud, wood and grass. Then, as the dirt road narrowed and grew rougher, the bus took them through great pineapple plantations stretching off on either side, the lush greenness reaching to the edge of the narrow track as they passed.

Finally, they arrived at a beautiful blue lagoon at the end of the road. There stood the African Queen, a small, old scow of a boat with a shed roof and an exposed engine, clattering furiously. Now everything came clear; Mr. and Mrs. Y *knew* that this was the real Africa because it looked so much like the photo in the brochure.

But no sooner were they secure in this image, than they were faced with a sudden and boisterous welcome. Around a point of land there appeared a small flotilla of motorboats each pulling a water skier, or rather whole, interlocking pyramids of water skiers, smiling and waving bright pennants, right out of an old Esther Williams spectacular.

Mr. and Mrs. Y wanted Africa to be like the Club Paradise brochure, but somehow it was *too* much like watching old movies or looking at a magazine. It was not quite real. Like Mr. and Mrs. K, they had not done enough prevacation work —sorting out how much of the real Africa they wanted, how much exploring, shopping, dealing with culture shock, and how much insulation by resort imagery they required. They had become mesmerized by an image and had great difficulty "translating" that image back into day-by-day plans.

Who (or What) Is to Blame?

This chapter has shown how guilt, separation anxiety and a variety of other responses can work to ruin a holiday. It has shown how they operate in three ways: by interfering with vacation planning, by combining with resentment to punish either the self or travel companions (or both), or else by a subconscious refusal to allow a bad experience or mood to turn into a good one.

From all this it should become clear that no outsider can spoil a person's vacation; it can only happen if that person is in collusion with the process and is simply giving enjoyment away. The spoiled vacation is a signal that the traveler is consumed by fears or guilt and is not managing to stay below what is called the *critical level of stress*. The spoiled vacation means that the time does not belong to the vacationer; it is the property of his or her inner fears and private demons.

CHAPTER SIX

🌺 *Putting It Together*

As we have been shown in previous chapters, there are vacation attitudes—both good and bad ones—and a variety of alternatives that can lead to happier vacations. The important thing now is for each person to assimilate these pieces of information and assume the responsibility of caring for the self and making the vacation into an experience of self-realization. One concrete way of doing this is to develop a log of your past holidays and a long-range projection of the future—a summary of what has been and a plan for what will be.

As you proceed, you will discover that the planning process itself is much more important than the specific ideas you evolve. Concentrating on what you want and need will focus your thoughts and make the whole business of time off seem far less haphazard—and hopefully filled with many more possibilities.

You will also discover that the time spent developing a log and plan of your vacations can help clarify those events that contribute to a successful holiday and those that lead to a bad one. By knowing the difference, it will be possible to shift the balance toward the good times.

The precise form of the following chart can of course be modified from individual to individual just as the projections you reach may be altered according to your later experience. Again, the most important thing is to establish a pattern of working for *yourself*, of giving a gift to yourself. The basic rule is: *share with others and be for yourself.*

A VACATION LOG

I. *Start a "Vacation Book" with a separate listing for each holiday in the past five years. Including comments on the following:*
   A. Location.
   B. Duration.
   C. Companion(s).
   D. Quality of the experience.
   E. Post-vacation feelings.

II. *Which category describes you best, and are you happy with it? Consider both past and present:*
   A. "It's better to have lived . . ."
   B. "Better safe than sorry."
   C. "If only I had followed my first impulse."
   D. "Things will always work out for the best."

III. *Consider your current "life style" period and the vacation characteristics associated with that period:*

Consult the life-cycle chart (see pages 18–19) and compare your vacation needs and desires with the characteristics ascribed to your age group. See also the table under IV.

IV. *Personal requirements:*

Here you should map out your own desires as you feel them now—and as you imagine they will be in years to come. The purpose of this table is to help clarify elements in your own personality that significantly influence your vacation pattern. Rate o (non-existent) to 4+ (very strong)

	Need Now	Need in Future	Never Need
Risk			
Excitement			
Intellectual stimulation			
Physical Activity			
Relaxation			
Togetherness			
Solitude			
Security			
Heritage			
Structure			
Improving Skills			
Status			
Luxury			
Shopping			

V. *Amount of money available for all vacations:*

Combining this with the previous findings will aid in determining just what is practically possible within the scope of your individual needs. If you want a vacation that is beyond your usual means, consider your budget in terms of one to four years. Cutting down a bit on expenses during other vacations may allow you that special trip. But don't fall into the trap of thinking you can forgo vacations completely one year because you'll make up for it next year.

A. This year.
B. Projected for the next two to three years.

VI. *Use of time:*

This part is much like the preceding in that it will help you discover just how the needs you have outlined above can best be met.

A. Total amount of vacation time available.
B. Division of that time into one long vacation, several shorter ones, or long weekends.
C. Division of time according to that spent alone, with spouse, with family, with friends.

VII. *Travel companion needs:*

	Now	Next Year	Following
Self			
Friends			
Family			
Tour			

VIII. *Special needs:*

>In this section you should consider any vacation requirements beyond your immediate desires, any special travel purpose you may see either now or in the future.
>A. Seeking a new home or business.
>B. Visiting relatives.
>C. Other.

IX. *Unfilled wishes, fantasies, or needs:*

>Now define these wishes and begin considering how vacations might best be used to fill these voids.

X. *Narrative description:*

>Compose a narrative description of yourself, both as you think you are now and as you imagine you will be in the future. Then share these conclusions with others (spouse, friends, etc.) for their reactions.

With the completion of this chart, you should have a coherent grasp of future trends within your own life. This will allow you to map out vacation priorities according to the goals you have set yourself.

Try to be farsighted and aware of the uses made of prior holidays if you are to avoid traveling as though last year never happened and next year will never come. By preparing this personal vacation book, you should gain a wider perspective from which holidays can be planned.

Once this log has been completed, the next step should be to use its information in future travel. The log has provided an assessment of your current emotional and social standing; a vacation plan built from it should guide you toward personal fulfillment.

Practically speaking, the plan should be developed for a

specific length of time. Prepare for several years in advance, carefully measuring your desires against your personality. If you can foresee a period of heavy stress in your business life, it might be wise to complement the period by planning a holiday of unstructured relaxation at that point, thus maintaining an inner balance.

By compiling this holiday planner, you will be investing as much forethought in your holiday as you do in other areas of your life. You will be treating vacationing as an instrument of self-realization. Which it is. The vacation experience is not a luxury, it is a necessity.

It is a challenge and an opportunity to enrich your personality. You can make your *time off* a true experience of self-renewal.

INDEX